THE ART OF SPARKLING

SHARE YOUR INNER LIGHT WITH THE WORLD

THE ART
OF
SPARKLING

SHARE YOUR INNER LIGHT WITH THE WORLD

BECKY BRITTAIN, PH.D.

Weeping Willow Books

ISBN 9978-1-7329706-4-9

Library of Congress Control Number 2020909081

Weeping Willow Books
Santa Barbara, CA

weepingwillowbooks.com

"*Think it not unimportant how*
you blaze the trail ahead
Or hold the guiding flame,
For always someone follows
where you go
And always someone comes
because you came."

— R.H. Grenville

"*O Thou Who giveth sustenance to the universe*
From Whom all things proceed,
To Whom all things return;
Unveil to us the face of the true spiritual Sun,
Hidden by a disc of golden light,
That we know the truth
And do our whole duty,
As we journey to Thy sacred feet."

— The Gayatri

Contents

FOREWORD

BECKY BRITTAIN is one of the most effervescent beings I have ever come across. I've never seen her down or in a low vibe, even in the midst of major health crises and global circumstances. She SPARKLES like no one I've ever met... truly. In fact I wouldn't hesitate to say she is the Queen of Sparklers the world over.

Becky is always up for the grandest work as a contribution to this world; she is a delight to collaborate with and to seek mastery from. I can't even imagine my life or this world without her in it.

The Art of Sparkling will take you into new horizons of who we are and how we can live, all together, as sparkling beings uplifting ourselves, the people around us and the world. You will discover your own masterful, sparkling Light in which you will dance brilliantly for yourself, your family and our world.

You'll learn new techniques as a master of sparkling and discover a way of living vibrantly, bringing your sparkling mastery to all of life around you—plants, people, environments, animals, everything.

With sparkling, everything glows and grows. Be prepared to be SPARKLED, reader, and welcomed into a version of reality for which you may have long yearned.

— Soleira Green, visionary and author, *The Real Art of Transformation* and other books

INTRODUCTION

*"Man is asked to make himself what he is
supposed to become to fulfill his destiny"*
— Paul Tillich

MY SUPERPOWER IS SPARKLING! I sparkle life. My passion is helping others shine more brightly. Sparkling is a transmission of energies visualized as sparkling light. I send out this radiant light through my fingers to intentionally enliven people, nature and animals. It's a dance in light!

As a sparkler, there is no need to carry a fairy wand, wield a light saber, or wear a superhero costume. Look inward. That's where your power lies. Each of us, in our core, has a "bare-naked radiance" that can be infused with more light. You have everything you need within you to sparkle. Cultivate your inner light and love. Amplify these energies, then project your light out for good. Become a sparkler in the spirit of love, for self-care, the nourishment of others, and to attract projects and prosperity. You can help create an amazing world with your light!

Webster's Dictionary defines sparkling as "to shine as if giving sparks." Magic is in the air when sparks of invisible light energies are extended to another to accelerate liveliness, happiness and joy. You connect to the pulse of life force that vibrates within you. Sparkling sends out life-enhancing energies as you magnify your inner light in alignment with Source. You can replenish others with bursts of radiance charged with a high frequency. Think of sparkling as a revitalizing energy source or as action prayer that utilizes light. Sparkling expresses your love, gratitude, wonder and delight.

Everyone can sparkle. Each one of us is a unique energetic being of light in a physical body. We are also connected to the electromagnetic energy fields of the earth. We all carry unrealized inner light that hold potentials to recharge life. Gary Zukav, in *The Seat of the Soul*, states: "the integrated human, the god-seed, is a being of laser light." Our educational system does not teach us how to amplify our vital forces, build up internal energetic powers, or share them with others. We can begin again to share a reciprocity with life.

Indigenous peoples were skilled at the art of moving energies to animate life. Shamans, kahunas, medicine men and masters cultivated their skills as quantum energy shifters. Our technological era does not emphasize using these arts to honor life as our ancestors did through sacred rituals and daily life-renewing practices.

Much of this dynamic information has been lost in modern times. Fortunately, energy/vibrational medicine is emerging in a breakthrough for wellness. We have energy workers and healing practitioners, as well as energy dowsers and martial artists who move energies. They are people who have taken the time to nurture their skills. We are not in the habit of giving back to the vitality of life. When Nature is seriously threatened, and our own bodies are overloaded by stress, sparkling honors and regenerates life. I believe sparkling comes from an ancient skill set that you can learn in a fresh way. It is time to restore this knowledge and make it available to both young and old as an everyday energetic resource.

Sparkling increases and accelerates your own internal light force to have an enlivening effect. Give this conscious gift to yourself, people, places and to all humanity. You will feel good charging up your own energies and using your sparkle powers. Sparkling fills you with energy and elevates your vibration, to expand your consciousness.

I have realized that my sparkling practice embodies what I learned from amazing teachers, who came across my path in each decade of my life. They guided me through important stages of personal growth to develop my knowledge and abilities. I was aware of their gifts to me at the time, but did not realize the deepening layers of knowledge I was receiving. As you will discover in this book, each teacher gave me another piece of the puzzle until it all fell into place. That was the day I realized the full potentials of sparkling as a powerful energetic tool for health and transformation.

My sparkling is a heart-felt, spontaneous practice that also reflects my spiritual awakening during a lifetime of learning and teaching adventures. Before becoming a serious sparkler, I shared my light, caring, knowledge and wisdom in various ways with my family, students and clients.

I am a mother and grandmother, with my doctorate in prenatal and perinatal psychology, who works as The Mothering Coach. I have supported many babies, children and parents, teaching about loving, touch, tenderness, bonding and family alchemy. I have been a registered dance-movement therapist and body-centered psychotherapist sharing the uplifting joy of movement and dance for health and mental health. I was an adjunct professor of somatic psychology at Washington University in St. Louis, where I taught about the unity of the body-mind-spirit connection.

These roles showed me that giving unconditional love to others increases both their vibration and my own. Then, a shift occurred in my professional counseling and coaching. I began to include energetic methods in my work to promote change by amplifying my clients' energies and consciousness. Energetic applications produced great results.

My sparkling first emerged spontaneously early in my twenties. I forgot about it for many years, until one day in 2010. I entered my husband's home office and noticed him hunched over at his desk and wondered what was wrong. He told me he was worried about business coming in. I wanted to help him somehow. Immediately I felt an inner impulse to sparkle him and asked him if I could. He said "sure" in a bemused and skeptical way. I sparkled away with wild abandon, using my hands, projecting large amounts of light through my fingertips. I transmitted intense sparkling energies to him that moved into his body, around his desk, and throughout the office space.

That day, I put my whole soul lovingly into this new act. Afterwards, I sensed the energies light up the room, making it look much brighter. Surprisingly, new business appeared quickly. It seemed connected. Then I started sparkling him and his business partner when they were pursuing more deals. These negotiations were successful. One day he said: "Honey, I am good. There's no need for sparkles today." We both laughed. At the time, I didn't really know what I was doing. On the surface, sparkling seemed like a simple act of communicating my caring. The more I did it, the more I felt that something deeper was going on. So, I extended my sparkling to myself, friends, clients, students, children and grandchildren, and to nature in all varieties and forms. Even people who didn't know what sparkling was liked the idea of it and asked me to sparkle them! Then, when I started getting good results, with folks asking for repeated sparkles, my curiosity was aroused. I began to wonder, "What is this sparkling all about?" "Who really is doing it?" "How does it work?"

Over time, I developed more sparkling mastery and began using it as my own spiritual practice. I now appreciate the simplicity, wonder and effectiveness of this approach. My sparkling has joyfully renewed the meaning of my entire life journey. It feels like a return home to the full magnificence of the Light that created me. It gives me the opportunity to shine more light back to others who may need it.

In my personal journey, I realize that beautiful divine sparks reside within all of us, like facets of diamonds. Sparkling can be a daily activity and spiritual practice to bring out your diamond-bright luminosity and make life glow.

Sparkling is a natural process and may also be your special talent. Many of us who are spiritually inclined people, creatives or energy workers clearly know we are here to help elevate the consciousness of humanity. During this unsettled period of history, sparkling brings light, energy and the frequency of hope.

Our world truly needs all the sparkles we can send out to bring out its living promise and potential. We can consciously become co-creators, working together to bring in new ways to vibrationally raise light for our planet for everyone. Sparkling can be used as a simple tool to inspire and uplift humanity in powerful ways. I want to help you discover its possibilities in your own life.

Do you want to assist the earth and her inhabitants
   by sharing your light?

Do you want to energize life, yourself and others?

Do you want to elevate frequencies and consciousness?

Do you want to bring in new positive changes?

In this book, you will learn ways to increase your inner light to sparkle yourself, family, friends, and your world. I will introduce ideas that support the art and science of sparkling with some original ideas to further your skills. You will be informed by my own spiritual journey and the special teachers who educated me about energy, flow, light, biofields and consciousness.

Think of this small book as a manual that will both inspire you and teach you to sparkle. From a lifetime of experience and study, it is clear to me that we are born to sparkle! It is a simple and beautiful gift to channel light through your fingers in creative ways for health and vitality and to benefit our world. It can evolve into a spiritual practice that supports your well-being. Your advanced mastery awaits you, which transforms your sparkling into fireworks. You emanate the sparkling presence. Sparkling is an energetic offering that is worth whatever time you can give to it.

"The creative process is not about trying or looking. It's about becoming your creation."

— Dr. Joe Dispenza

WHAT IS SPARKLING?

"Travel light, live light, spread the light, be the light."

—Yogi Bhajan

ALL HUMAN BEINGS CARRY VITAL ENERGIES of resplendent light within. Use sparkling to learn about yourself as a person who holds light with its full regenerative potentials. It's a way to discover your full superpower birthright. A sparkler sends showers of light, rippling with sparkling energies, that flow out of the hands and fingers to whomever or whatever you want. Sparkles flicker and vibrate as living spirit! You release your life force in a healthy way.

The key to great sparkling is the winning combination of your clear intent, heart connection, and energetic application, aligned with Source or the quantum field of consciousness. This practice makes use of our generally unknown abilities to vibrationally boost life to a higher frequency. Sparkle from a wealth of unlimited possibilities that are literally in your heart and hands. I have discovered that sparkling is a simple act of caring in divine service. As Fred Rogers affirms: "I am always comforted by realizing that there are still so many helpers, so many caring people in the world."

Sparkling has many purposes. Use it to:

Connect to renewing infinite Source of energies.

Bless and honor the recipient to generate a feeling of well-being.

Boost energy to build a stronger life force.

Raise all frequencies of life.

Send out unconditional love to activate joy.

Share light with the world.

Focus your intention to direct your sparkling. (i.e. to clear negative energies).

Transmit energies of love, peace, freedom, beauty, abundance and happiness.

Animate mind, body, spirit, and soul for wellness and regeneration.

Promote evolutionary shifting.

Just as each snowflake is unique, sparkles are ever-changing. You actively create sparkles from the quality and potency of your inner light, fueled by your intention, and infused by your sheer joy. Visualizing this light adds greatly to the power of this creative alchemical mix. Imagine each iridescent sparkle as containing radiant crystalline and diamond properties. When you offer sparkling as a celebratory exchange, you create radiance filled with magical possibilities, potency, and oomph that may restore health, purpose and well-being.

There is great benefit when you seek out a new path to develop untapped internal resources that meaningfully engage your soul. Try sparkling and feel its joy, effervescence and power! Let your imagination inspire you to find more ways to shine and make shifts for others.

Sparkling can be offered anytime and cultivated by anyone as a personal resource or skill. It may develop into a deep spiritual practice, be used to uplift others, or just be a lot of fun. Everyone has different experiences with sparkling. There are so many factors that may influence your personal impact. Become a ray of pure light to share your goodness with the world.

The essential gift of sparkling is that it continuously raises your own light vibration. You immediately feel energized and can extend waves of sparkling light to raise others up with a blessing or quickening boost. Your body then adjusts to accept a higher vibrational setpoint. Sparkle yourself to replenish your energy reserves, when you feel like your light is dimmed, or your energies are lowered. Sparkle up to help yourself when you feel downhearted or fatigued.

Sparkling came to me intuitively as a spontaneous expression. It has been fun to discover and explore this dormant ability that exists within us all. At first glance, some people might consider sparkling as silly, but nothing could be further from the truth. It is not about glitz or glamour, but about making a caring engagement with another, while offering unconditional love with energetic enhancement!

Sparkling is transformative, not a frivolous or superficial distraction. It's a natural expression of light given with pure love and dedication. Who doesn't need an extra sparkle "a la mode" now and then for greater joy? Or when fatigued, depleted, or disheartened? Albert Schweitzer inspired me when he said: "At times our own Light goes out and is rekindled by a spark from another person. Each of us has cause to think with deep gratitude of those who have lighted the flame in us." Sparkling is an everyday blessing to life.

Become a sparkler! We embody light and are continuously surrounded by fields of light that provide life-sustaining energies. You can tap into these energies that permeate your physical body into your light body. Your skills grow exponentially with practice and empower change on many levels. These sparkling effects move quantumly to uplift frequencies creating expansive fields of light, where they are consciously directed.

Sparkling is meant to be restorative and is not intended as a healing modality. There are many other energetic techniques available specifically for these purposes. Massage therapists, energy healers, Healing Touch and Reiki practitioners offer their hands-on talents for direct therapeutic work. Sparkling is an uplifting tool that increases vital forces and creates energetic shifts. It can supplement other healing approaches, by providing delight and offering tender ways to lift moods and improve life force. This approach, validated by science, is my professional and loving contribution to the well-being of humanity.

As a sparkler, I welcome every request for a light transmission. It is my joy to sparkle. It can't hurt and you just might create some fantastic results. The famous quote by Shakespeare applies: "There are more things in heaven and earth, Horatio, than are dreamt of in your philosophy."

My good friend's daughter in her mid-twenties always requests sparkling when she visits. She has asked me to sparkle her for career advancement, a perfect overseas job, abundance and a new love interest, and she has since manifested all of this. She is always quite enthusiastic to be sparkled. I give it my best, because it's fun to empower her infinite prospects.

One time, I began by sending her a huge burst of sparkles to enlarge her own energy field. I then transmitted sparkles directly into her body, to establish more energetic circulation. Sensing some dark or gray areas within her light field, I cleared them out with a quick flick and then filled her up with bright golden light. I sparkled her front and back, moving in a clockwise direction around her body. Energies were moved up her spine along her back and then sent down the front of the body. Finally, I sensed her true magnificence and sent her waves of light to boost the realization of her amazing potentials.

After the sparkling, she looked radiant and luminous. She said she experienced a huge surge of light-filled clarity and confidence and felt liberated from doubts about herself. She felt affirmed for the bright light that she is!

Everyone appreciates receiving this magical form of blessing. Sparkling produces a sense of joyful, wondrous awe, and never a sense of energetic depletion. You intuitively know when to sparkle and under what circumstances to shine your light, or you don't do it.

For best results, don't sparkle someone when you are emotionally down or sick. Set the intention to be directly aligned to higher consciousness or a Greater Source of energy that orchestrates what is best for that person to receive. If they give permission, then there is a go-ahead to sparkle and the moment is right.

The benefits of sparkling vary with the need. Sparkling can either soothe a worried mind, or energize the body, or profoundly raise spirits! Envision the hand-held sparklers that you bring out for Fourth of July celebrations. They burn slowly and emit sparkles of white or colored light. We wave them to celebrate the light of freedom, but mostly for their fun and kaleidoscopic sparkling effect.

Imagine that you share the invisible gift of sparkling through your fingers. Shine your light brightly. Upgrade your wondrous abilities and commit to sparkling.

> *"Let's sparkle and spark; let's be as wild and free as our energy wishes us to be; let's flow to whatever this love of being directs us."*
>
> — Soleira Green

How to Sparkle

*"Often the hands solve a mystery that the
intellect has struggled with in vain."*

— C. J. Jung

THE MAIN PURPOSE OF SPARKLING is to send out your inner light
to yourself and others, when your heart is touched to do so.
The sparkler uses high vibrational frequencies received in
his/her body and energetic fields from a variety of sources.
Although you do not see sparkles of light moving out from
your fingers, trust the process.

Be certain and strong in your belief that you will become
a good sparkler! Summon your whole being, especially your
heart, to move you in this enlightened direction. Step into the
light and know that your journey, no matter the route taken,
is perfect for you! Try sparkling anything and practice and
play with it.

As you learn ways to sparkle, pay attention to what feels
pleasurable and works for you. It's up to you to discover the
simple wonders of sparkling; sparkling takes on a life of its

own as you discover new applications. There are no specific rules. Start it up and feel its joy and power!

Hopefully, my description of sparkling will allow you to engage in a process that offers you an experience of magic and meaning. I will orient you to the basics of the process and describe how to sparkle in different ways. You will receive my thoughts about those aspects and characteristics that make sparkling unique. Lastly, I will provide you with valuable suggestions that have helped me sparkle effectively. This advice is not meant to be overly directive, but rather to share ideas that have worked best for me as a sparkler. Your own experience is what matters.

There are many ways to approach sparkling. Here are some basic suggestions to get you started.

PREPARING TO SPARKLE:

Start by grounding and charging your energies.

Stand comfortably with your body relaxed, knees flexible and spine aligned.

Plant your feet firmly in the ground to access earth energies.

Breathe deeply several times to switch on your full bodily power.

Connect the energies of the earth with the energies of the sun above your head. Keep breathing continuously to fully charge up.

Feel the potent light-charge of the sun that is absorbed inside your body and cells. (You do not have to be standing out in the sun.)

Send moving energies, infused with light, up and down your body and then to your heart center. Connect to the magnificence of your divine spark to achieve a higher vibrational alignment.

Wiggle your fingers. Rub your hands together to increase light concentration in your hands.

THE ACT OF SPARKLING:

Hold out your hands and move your fingers to direct light beams with effervescent sparkles. Practice doing this with a flowing or a flicking movement, transmitting successive sparks. Place your awareness on whomever or whatever you are sparkling and direct your aim like an archer, or like a fairy sending out fairy dust. Make sure you are connected to the highest frequency energies that direct and guide you to new levels. Feel your light shining within and without to bestow exactly what is needed.

Sparkling is both a simple act and a deep, multifaceted practice with many aspects. Here are some:

SPARKLING IS AN ENERGETIC TRANSMISSION. Allow invisible energies of love and bright light to flow out of the hands and through the fingers. Energies move to the one who receives it. It is all about sending the most expansive energies as shimmering sparkles.

SPARKLING IS A DANCE OF LIGHT. Move your hands, fingers and body fluidly and lightly in the air. Sparkling carries the spirit of expressive dancing. I imagine myself as a light dancer, or an alert and nimble ninja who is masterfully flexible in every motion and gesture.

The expressive movement of my body and hands stirs forces to charge up the light that you, then, can transmit in many creative ways. I love to sparkle continuously and rhythmically as I walk. I move and sway my hips, jauntily sparkling all of things that my eye and senses behold. I try to mix up my sparkling movements from soft to strong, small to large, slow to quick, staccato to flowing. Sparkling can be applied gently as a light touch or as sweeping waves of energies that provide a tapestry of light over a large area.

SPARKLING IS AN ACT OF LOVE. Navigate through your world and notice anything that touches your heart that you wish to sparkle. You may feel awe or appreciation or gratitude and want to accentuate that, or you may feel moved to help others, restore something, or spark more love in it.

SPARKLING IS PLAY. Sparkle spontaneously. Energies flow easily from your hands like water flowing from a spout or like a breath of fresh air. Delight in the *joie de vivre* of the present moment. You don't need a wand, but you can use one if that makes the experience more fun for you.

SPARKLING IS INTUITIVE. Listen to knowing that comes from within…a nudge from the heart or gut, or just a kinesthetic sensing about what is appropriate and worthwhile. (Sometimes, my fingertips tingle to indicate that a sparkling is needed.) Move between your inner and outer worlds to tune into your own intuition that reflects your higher self. This connects you directly to your internal wisdom about what is best for each sparkling. Honor these intuitions.

SPARKLING IS EXTRAORDINARY. Go beyond yourself and be surprised as you may feel that the spirit of sparkling takes you into a magical world or worlds. You may observe unexpected colors, features or details of life, or experience the awe of being immersed in another light-filled dimension of cosmic sparkles. Positive occurrences, synchronicities and/or outcomes can't be predicted.

Your imagination inspires creative ideas and experiences for new sparkling explorations. Improvise and keep an open heart to avoid over-thinking. Allow your thoughts to drift like the snow in a snow globe, so your mind can become still. Sparkling is a right-brain activity that is creative, rather than logical. Allow it to take you on novel adventures and into undiscovered realms of light.

SPARKLING IS AN ENERGETIC MAGNIFIER. Amplify energies through sparkling applications of light sent to whatever is needed to influence beneficial change and growth. This transmission is received in both the physical body and the subtle bodies and energy fields. Charge up all your prospects using sparkling, carrying the intended focus to manifest health, wellness and prosperity with a lifestyle you desire.

SPARKLING WORKS LONG DISTANCE. Know that time and space are irrelevant because we live in a quantum world with infinite, limitless possibilities. Sparkles can be sent to any place or person in the world with the same effects as if done in person. You can sparkle others solely in your imagination, without a physical gesture. Your sparkling may reach up to the stars to those loved ones who have passed on, and they might reciprocate the gesture and sparkle you back in return.

SPARKLING IS A CO-CREATIVE CONNECTION. Give and receive in the dancing dialogue between two unique souls. As you meet and greet another, each person is truly seen and witnessed, and each other's light is reflected and enhanced. This is a transpersonal connection on physical, emotional, energetic and ethereal levels. You may notice that awareness expands from this alchemical exchange. Vibrant connections of energies can light up intertwining biofields and sometimes electric fireworks are felt through the energetic interaction.

Here are some helpful suggestions to consider as you sparkle:

ASK PERMISSION TO SPARKLE ANOTHER IN PERSON. Be sensitive not to energetically invade someone's personal space or surprise them. This creates boundaries and a sense of trust for personal safety. If they give personal permission, go-ahead and sparkle. When sparkling another, make eye contact and smile to establish a good connection.

ACCESS PRIMARY SOURCES OF ENERGIES. Inexhaustible energies and unfathomable amounts of light are always available to the sparkler. They originate from quantum Power Source points both inside and outside of you. You will discover your own best power source(s) and can use all of them. Experiment with ways to call on or access the best energies for you! Summon your own sparks of infinite light and love. Align with the sun's rays. Do you have a spiritual orientation? You may call on Source, The Prime Creator, Oneness, Christ Consciousness or your favorite spiritual teacher to assist you. However, you may already embody the light you need.

You can tap into a "sparkling" frequency that emits the most dazzling light! Imagine this glittering frequency with all your senses, as an effervescent sparkling fountain or diamond bright waterfall. It is always available to stream through you, to be transmitted to others. There are many other light flames, forcefields and frequencies, like those of Love, Truth, and Wisdom, that you can use for good purposes.

RAISE THE VIBRATION. Become dedicated to continually raise your personal light and energy vibration. Sparkle yourself with light. Visualize sending bright sparkles that also carry the currents of happiness and joy to another. Do not take on another's low vibrational energy. Allow your higher vibration to be the primary uplifting frequency. When you combine your love and light together, the potency of your broadcast is amplified. You feel buoyant and laugh a lot as a sparkler.

SET CLEAR INTENTIONS. Fuel your sparkling process with your clearest intent to bring clarity and focus. Your foremost intention is that your sparkling will only benefit life and never hurt anyone or anything. The receiver may ask for an energy boost, loving appreciation, or energetic support for financial flow, etc. Listen to these personal desires and intend to fulfill them but stay open for something even more amazing to happen!

Communicating mutual intentions greatly enhances the effectiveness of the sparkling. Co-create with the universe to send out the best possible sparks of light. Charge up sparkling with positive emotions that add zing to the alchemical mix meant to align with your highest ideals and highest intentions.

STAY NEUTRAL IN EXPECTATIONS. Stay unattached to outcomes. Listen and understand what needs to happen but surrender to the highest good. Get out of your own way. No one has control over how the transmission will be used by the person or by the Divine. "Let go, let God" is the perspective that is best for a sparkler to hold. Imagine yourself as an open and clear channel for Greater Light to flow through you. Sparkling doesn't come from a place of trying to be loved, or accepted by others, nor from a place of superiority, wishing to save or rescue another.

HONOR THE SPIRIT OF SPARKLING. Focus on the bright, illuminating, happy, spirit of sparkling and how this wants to flow through you. Sparkles can be given formally or informally without overly drawing attention to yourself. Sparkling is a precious gift that may be given and received with gratitude.

Sparkling is a new-generation energetic approach that is fun, subtle, powerful and easy to do. Your physical body is connected to the vast quantum fields of energies. Sparkling boosts these vital energies where and when they are needed for purposes of health, well-being and consciousness expansion. You can easily learn how to sparkle, enjoy it, and apply sparkling to give more pizzazz to life. The alchemy of light and love can pour through your fingers with intention and imagination. Become aware of energy dynamics inside you and around you to access a full powerhouse of different high frequencies available for your sparkling brilliance and effectiveness. The great news is that sparkling brings light-hearted pleasure and self-confidence that can be applied to all areas of your life, and in service to many.

> *"Finding the light and cultivating it, so that it shines ever stronger through the physical body and the Body of Light, is that vertical reaching out which links us back to our home in no-time no space."*

> — Dona Holleman, *Dancing the Body of Light*

WHO AND WHAT TO SPARKLE?

*"We cannot live only for ourselves. A thousand
fibers connect us with our fellow man."*

— Herman Melville

SPARKLING IS A GREAT TOOL for practicing random acts of
kindness. Your intuition picks up when these may be needed.
Choose to become someone's sparkling angel, fairy, or muse.
Sparkle to your heart's content, as there are so many reasons
to do it. Whom or what do you want to sparkle? Transmit
your sparkles to light up yourself, others, animals and the
world. Sparkling is basically an altruistic expression. The
good news is that it does support others, who then ask for your
assistance. You in turn receive positive energetic currents
back from your sweet actions.

Sparkling yourself is a great way to begin. I follow the
airline rule of putting your oxygen mask on first before
helping others. You can send sparkles to yourself from head
to toe either by physical flicking or your imagination alone.
Repeat the action again to reinforce the strength and potency
of sparkles that you receive. This self-sparkling can be gentle

31

or robust and filled with potential of marvelous results that enhance your mastery. Fill yourself completely with a great light infusion. It's like pouring milk into a pitcher to the brim. Intend this. If you feel the light is not sparkly enough, empty out the old light and start over until you feel effervescent. Now you have uplifted your sparkling to life.

Sparkling your plants is very easy to begin. No one watches you doing this, so you don't need to feel self-conscious. You can build up your confidence in your abilities until you feel bold enough to sparkle people. It is fun to watch your plants respond to your sparkling attention. It is nice to start by saying hello. This is a polite greeting that alerts them that you are present and would like to interact. Wake up their intelligence by making a conscious heartfelt connection, which is essential for communion. Then energetic conduits of both you and the plants are open and inviting for the sparkling process to be received. Watch and see how your plants respond to your sparkling. Do you feel their engagement with you? Can you see any results over time? How do you feel about the process of doing something new? If you follow through with dedication, you will begin to see changes. Remember your sense of your own progress is filtered by your perceptions. Getting amazing results is not the focus for your sparkling. You want the process to be enjoyable.

When I started sparkling trees, shrubs, and plants around my front door, there was a continuous buildup of energetic support given to the plants that later appeared as a kind of overall glow at the entrance. Many visitors to my house reported they could feel or sense this magical emanation. The plants were beautiful and flourishing. Try sparkling your indoor and outdoor plants, shrubs, flowers and your vegetable garden. You will probably notice that the plants look healthier and might show a growth boost. I have so many blooms that we can hardly get out of the door. My husband wondered if I had over-sparkled them! Sometimes I notice the plants leaning into me, for that extra soak of love and added glimmering light sent their way, which makes me feel happy.

Sparkle and hug trees in your community. They actively communicate with you, sending out so much wisdom and love in return for the favor. I wonder if any human has sparkled the plants at magical Findhorn, besides the fairies who supposedly reside there. Recently, I noticed the impact of my sparkling habit. We moved down the street and I changed my walking route. The roses that I used to sparkle every day, and which flourished with such radiant glow, were now drooping and forlorn with no blooms. It had been months since I had walked by and sparkled them. I apologized for my sudden leaving with no advance warning. Now I sparkle them long distance as they had become my friends that I cannot leave behind. I walked past them last week to check on them and there was some regrowth with a beautiful bloom!

The more you can create a loving and sacred relationship with Nature, the better. Nature is alive and supports you endlessly through vital interconnections in the web of life. You share the elements of earth, wind, fire and water with it. It also requires your reciprocal conscious care, nurture, and appreciation. Sparkle to extend the beauty of nature that you observe. When Nature thrives, it continually replenishes and refuels your own sparkle power. We all know the revitalizing impact that being in Nature can bring with exposure to its enriching oxygen, biodiversity, beautiful colors, shapes and subtleties. "Grounding" research tells us that the earth carries powerful electromagnetic life-enhancing energies. Try walking barefoot when you are sparkling outdoors to charge yourself up!

As a conscious, living being, Nature lovingly invites your synergy to help upgrade mutual frequencies. Reciprocally, you can become motivated to send the "pulse of life" back to the nature spirits who may be inhabiting your land. My friend and teacher, the dowser Raymon Grace, shared the idea that, if these nature spirits are not present, then you really need to move energies to help them return. As you practice your skills, you'll get a feel for the levels of effervescence or depletion in the plants or natural areas around you. Find a spot that appears energetically depleted by human neglect and misuse, then sparkle it repeatedly, until you can see or feel the natural life force return. Your energetic support may help restore it back to its former vitality and glow. How beneficial to serve the elementals and Nature in such a loving way, during this time of climate change with so many environmental concerns.

Sparkle your pets! They appreciate and feel every ministration. Studies suggest that human interaction resonates within the biofields of animals to create an ongoing connection that is highly beneficial to both owners and their pets. Our pets intuitively know how to love and comfort their loved ones and use their intelligence beyond words. Dogs sparkle their appreciation with their loving eyes, touch, cuddles and wagging tails. Cats lay on their back and purr to express bliss. My friend's dog, Louie, is a sparkle lover who prefers to sleep on the sofa's sparkly sequin pillow. Sparkle the wild animals at the zoo! It makes me happy when I see species returning to their habitats, rather than being extinguished from the planet. Let's sparkle to preserve the diversity of the animal and plant kingdoms!

Extend sparkling nurture to all children, who are young, tender, growing shoots of life. You can use your energies of light to do this in a subtle way, during their impressionable earliest years. They feel loved and understood when a respectful person deeply honors them with a special sparkling moment. Let them know what you wish to do and ask if they would like to be sparkled. Be very gentle and loving in your approach. Watch the effects and be careful not to overstimulate their sensitive nervous systems. At night, you can sparkle children and members of your family along with offering them prayers, in person or long distance. I do this routinely in the presence of my own grandchildren, who now sparkle their friends. The universe really supports these prayerful requests and your beneficial actions to have all persons loved and protected for their highest good. Sparkle the kids who live in your neighborhood or the refugee kids at a distance and all children around the planet. Sparkle sick children. When I worked as a dance therapist in hospitals, I sparkled children with cancer to enliven their radiant souls with divine joy. They loved receiving all the sparkles and often asked for their parents to receive them as well, which was touching to me. Of course, I sparkle all babies to welcome them into the world and give a sparkle boost to their exhausted parents. Sparkling can become an honoring ritual for birth, death, birthdays and other special occasions and ceremonies. It brings a sense of celebration though the power of love.

Most of your sparkling will be sent to your family, friends and acquaintances. We live in uncertain times and everyone is going through either stress, disappointment, or challenges with their health, deaths of friends and loved ones, relationships, or finances, or knows someone who is. Sparkling offers hope because it sends out positive energies and light to help energize infinite possibilities. I love to sparkle new life transitions, like pregnancy, first days of school, college acceptance, jobs, and career moves. I went into a store and the owner asked me to sparkle her son-in law because he had been laid off and has a family. I did not need to ask his permission, because I had sparkled him before at his request. I sent an arc of radiating sparkles over three counties to encourage his new job prospects. It felt like this sparkle offering helped this job finding situation. Sparkles are a great way to help someone when words are not enough.

Sparkle all helping professionals and staff in hospitals, with their consent if possible. They need the upgrade of positive vibrations, expressed with tenderness and compassion. Burnt-out nurses and tired caregivers, whose light may be dimmed, are especially receptive and grateful for an elevation in frequency. Sparkle the patients too, with their permission. You can kindly say, "May I offer you some sparkles today?" I sparkled my husband every day during a long hospital stay to help boost his immune system. Please sparkle all elders and teachers in schools. The power to boost spirits using this life-affirming way is so appreciated!

Sparkling has endless practical applications. Sparkle your cooking to infuse a wonderful mix of healthy ingredients, spices and love. Sparkle your food to bless it before you eat. This expression of gratitude before it enters your body adds to its nutritional vibrancy as well as an artistic expression. Sparkle your writing, art, photographs, projects, and your computers for enlightening ideas to add vibrancy to your creative expression. I have sparkled this manuscript to uplift you! Sparkle your professional work and important emails and conversations that you wish to be received well. If you are doing a home construction project, sparkle to bless the workers and materials that will be involved in creating a new environment for you. Sparkle your favorite sports teams! Sparkle your investments and money in your billfold to create more abundance and embody that golden emanation. I subtly sparkle my playing cards when playing gin rummy with my husband and I usually win! Sparkle traveling passengers in buses and airports exposed to low-level frequencies. The list is limitless. You get the idea. Who or what do you want to start sparkling?

Sparkling can help to clear negative, dense or heavy energies. For example, big box stores really need it. I always sparkle myself in these environments. There can be a concentration of compressed energies from crowds and the oppressive effects of the fluorescent lights. Often, you can feel these chaotic energies that cause your vibration to suddenly drop. You can clear them, in a very subtle way, so no one ever notices. Hold your arms down and sparkle close to the ground. I am often asked to clear bad energies in a meeting room or to remove and flick away negative energies received from hurtful conversations or negative, aggressive people. Sparkle to remove any non-beneficial energies that maybe be present in your body or home and then do a re-sparkle to fill that area with positive energies. Feel the difference. Next, sparkle yourself if you have picked up anything that has lowered your frequency. Becoming aware of energy depletion and then replenishing it is key to retaining a sparkling presence. You obviously need to fundamentally choose a new self-care option that embraces filling yourself up with light and love. In another chapter, you will learn about ways to use sparkling to revitalize your health for increased vitality.

Let's use sparkling to raise the light in our cells, selves, homes, communal spaces and communities. You can sparkle to restore goodness, purity, charity, faith, courage and hope. You can sparkle to clear the effects of energetic depletion so prevalent in our society. Help restore the balance and harmony that is our birthright. The idea is to animate life with Divine sparks to also move us forward for favorable evolutionary, environmental and spiritual outcomes.

The big takeaway of this book is that you have powers of light as human gifts that are largely not used. The spark of light that lives inside of you is meant to be consciously used for the good and help you express your quantum magnificence. Stay aligned to continuously cultivate your strong, steady and peaceful glowing light. Then you can beam out a luminous flame from your self-created safe harbor of self-calm and peace. The true gift of sparkling is the quality of light and others. You are learning how easy it is to bring small changes through sparkling that revitalize and restore yourself and other beings in a tender, subtle way. Use your gifts.

"For every atom belonging to me as good belongs to you."

-—— Walt Whitman

THE SOURCE OF SPARKLING

*"Ultimately light is the mother of life. Where
there is no light, there can be no life."*

— John O' Donohue

THE SUN IS THE SOURCE of all light on earth. It showers our
planet with moving wavelengths and particles of light.
Sparkling originates from these energies that make all life
possible. Light is the artful medium for sparkling. Sparkling is
an energetic tool that mirrors the first act of God, who chose
the medium of light for creation.

The Bible tells us how the first light was transmitted by
God to create and animate all life: "And God said, Let there be
light and there was light." (Genesis 1:3). Sparkling, magnified
by love, replicates this most wondrous compassionate act
of giving life. The living stream of sparkles that you send
reflects an intimate sacred transmission of an invisible God
Power that is yours to have and use.

Michelangelo's beautiful painting on the ceiling of the
Sistine Chapel, called "The Creation of Adam," symbolically
portrays the moment when God gave life to the first man.

The Prime Creator extends his finger to Adam, releasing vital energies to animate him and give him consciousness. As viewers, we are moved by the transmission of the invisible universal spark.

We intuitively know that the divine spark, that lives within our heart, is the sacred fire of inner light that illuminates thought, consciousness and ignites heart-felt love with contagious enthusiasm. It helps to ignite all the other invisible light energies in our body and surrounding it, known as the aura. All these light energies are intelligent and miraculously coalesce to continuously inform our being and soul about the nature and conditions of our inner and outer world. Energies of light exist everywhere. This energy provides life force that is pervasive and life-sustaining.

Know that your unique Divine spark, which can access your divine soul's purpose and blueprint, unfolds perfectly at its own pace inside of you. Trust that it will spark your uniqueness, passions, and potentials at the right moment. This may transcend your conscious awareness. As a sparkler, pause in stillness to meditate on the beauty and divine depths of this glorious light flame. Rowena Pattee Krowder, in *Sacred Ground to Sacred Space*, wrote, "The vital force of our bodies is transformed into *illumined* consciousness."

Every day since the dawn of humanity, we have looked up at the sun, moon and stars with wonder. You reflect this wondrous light! History tells us that early humans were sun worshippers. These wise ancient ancestors revered the light of the sun and held ceremonies to sustain and honor the sacredness of life in service for the good of the whole.

This deep partnership with light, connection to nature and the Source of all was revered, and not taken for granted. American Indian and other indigenous cultures have early myths and stories and practices that celebrate light as the prime ingredient of creation. The Plains Indians created their Sun Dance, the Incas had rituals to their sun God called Inti, and the all-pervading powers of Ra were celebrated by the Egyptians.

Spiritual teachers, from different religious traditions through the ages, have shared messages of light and love that inspire us to lead lives in service to our creator and to each other. There are many spiritual celebrations of light held annually across the planet, including Diwali, a Hindu festival of lights; Candlemas, a Christian tradition; Kwanzaa, an African-American tradition; Hanukkah, an important Jewish celebration; Bon Matsui, a Buddhist tradition in Japan; and Saint Lucia Day in Sweden, to name a few. These rituals around the world focus on the power, gifts and mysteries of light that inspire our psyches and souls.

Science has put the energies of light on the forefront in the modern era. According to quantum physics, energies of light eternally fill the universe in a cosmic dance of oscillating waves and fields. Our physical bodies seem solid to us, but they actually consist of space and quanta, packets of light that create a bioelectrical field in and around your body, which we call the aura.

Everything in the Universe is light and energy, whose sparks and impulses nourish our brain, draw subtle energy into our chakras and bodies, and allow us to see. About ninety percent of all information that we receive about our world is conveyed by light that enters our eyes. The retina sends information to the brain, which decodes it into visual images. Our visual cortex is the route to our imaginative capabilities. The third eye has the capacities for inner spiritual vision. Our meridians are "networks of energy channels." Light affects the balance of energies in the hypothalamus region of our brains and can influence the self-regulation of our feelings and thoughts.

As a sparkler, you can serve as a powerful messenger and conduit of light who sends and receives sparkles that can have beneficial impacts. Your awareness assists this process. Every person's electromagnetic fields and frequencies are constantly changing and in flux in relation to internal and external factors. We live in relation to a sea of light fields, bodies, and beings of light that carry their own qualities and frequencies of light. Your own thoughts, emotions, bodily states and ongoing experiences may carry higher or lower vibrations from these inputs. Your personal light may vary in purity, intensity and direction of service at different moments.

The language of the universe is frequency. Nikola Tesla said: "If you want to understand the secrets of the universe, think in terms of energy, frequency and vibration." The essential question for sparklers is this: Are you broadcasting a harmonic or disharmonic light pattern? The choice is yours. Pay close attention to the vibration of your energies, to the level of your consciousness, to the quality of your thoughts and to the words you speak. Cultivate the quality of your personal light and its expansion!

Your energetic frequencies can become lowered by depleting factors, such as illness, anxiety, sadness, stress, light deprivation, and poor nutrition and by energies in the collective. Discover ways to discern your present energetic state and make positive adjustments in your frequency to create harmonies to elevate your mood and health. Are you exposing yourself to people and situations that carry a high vibration to increase your happiness, health and well-being? Choose to surround yourself with the highest vibrations possible to create resonate waves within your being. Others immediately pick up when your energies look bright and your vibration is higher.

Think of yourself as a deejay. Sparkling is your superpower to raise and modulate the frequencies and energies of the light you emit. Create your own electrifying and exhilarating mix every day. Go to your core and imaginatively spin your cells to sparkle at a higher rate for well-being, joy and happiness. Use this constant awareness to enliven your physical energies and raise the vibrations of your being to benefit yourself and others.

We are currently shifting from a mechanistic scientific paradigm to a quantum one, which is creating the momentum to propel us into an Age of Light. As co-creators with the collective family of light, we may once again value the sacred gifts we have been given, like our indigenous ancestors did. We can use our intrinsic light powers in new imaginative ways to become sunshine for others in our world. This can greatly serve our planetary awakening.

"If all starlight and sunlight were visible,
we could behold the pathways of light that
are the architecture of the universe."

— Rowena Pattee Krowder

Sparkling Inspirations

"If you want your children to be intelligent, read them fairy tales. If you want them to be more intelligent, read them more fairy tales."

— Albert Einstein

INSPIRATIONS FOR SPARKLING are everywhere! There are so many unseen sparkling messengers, who actively bring light to our world. Work with them. Look for your own guides, who may come from higher divine realms or other sources, like dreams, legends, literature and animals. I want to share with you some of my sparkling influencers, both serious and fun. Consider them and you will find your own enduring and momentary inspirations. The wonderful thing is that when you sparkle you draw closer to the light reflected within all beings.

Sparkling is a Divine Art of angelic origin that offers spiritual focus to let the light in. Angels are portrayed with the splendor of sparkling halos and iridescent wings. Their light bodies transmit forcefields of pure light and love to us serving in continual ministry. Archangel Uriel, whose name means "God's Light" brings the clarity of Light to all situations, especially unpleasant ones. When we ask for help or healing, selfless angels invisibly and sweetly caress us. Many times, I have called on them and have felt genuinely restored and sparkled.

Like the angels, enlightened beings and teachers from different religious and spiritual traditions have been visually portrayed with magnificent coronas of light around their heads. According to Richard Rudd in his book, *Gene Keys*, there are many accounts of masters in Egyptian, Taoist, and Tibetan traditions "who attained the body of Light or the rainbow body," which involved transcending usual physical laws. Christ was one of these teachers who received his full light body after the crucifixion, when he appeared able to rematerialize his form to his disciples after death. He brought amazing teachings of Light to humanity. He is often depicted with a corona, which signifies a very high level of alchemical light mastery and spiritual liberation. The Bible quotes the Lord as saying, "Therefore, if your whole body is full of light, and no part of it dark, it will be just as full of light, as when a light shines its light." (Luke11:36). This verse has inspired my desire to acquire increasing levels of full body radiance: "There are many beings amongst you who have developed the ability to conduct heightened electromagnetic frequencies through the vehicle of their physical forms." (Rasha, *Oneness*).

Many people pray to Mary, the mother of Jesus, whose purity and loves eternally blesses us selflessly. She is a holy, luminous and benevolent saint. Paintings usually depict her with a sacred heart that radiates light. It has been recorded that she has appeared to children and other followers in visions as a sparkling presence of light sharing her profound miraculous love. The Feminine aspect of God, the Divine Mother, is the ultimate Sparkler, who nurtures all life, birthed from her sacred womb. She is the Source of Creation who brings guidance, love and light to all who remember Her. She has seeded us with the breath of life, conscious intelligence, compassionate hearts and souls, within the divinity of beautiful bodies, glowing light bodies, genes, and our DNA.

Sparkling facets of light from different spiritual traditions and realms bring teachers who move our collective hearts. Many spiritual masters throughout history have taught about the importance of light and love to guide your actions to act with unconditional compassion. Your specific religious tradition and spiritual orientation do not matter if you are a sparkler. Although all beings embody light, each teacher has a unique quality of light. Think about who or what lights you up and inspires you to act with unconditional loving compassion.

Because Light is fundamental to life, it is a universal symbol to mankind, held within the collective unconscious and archetypal realms that reveal the ultimate reality. For example, in America we revere the light bearing torch of freedom held by the Statue of Liberty. In the opening ceremonies of the Olympics, runners representing all nations of the world carry and pass along a torch that lights the breath-taking central caldron of fire that burns until the closing ceremony. I think this reflects a Spiritual Light whose attributes are wisdom, goodness, purity, and truth. Don't we want to become a beacon of Light for others to change the world? Can the power of collective sparkling change the course of humanity's consciousness for the greater good?

Sparkling has played a part in many legends and stories. For example, folklore, fairytales, art and movies have engaged us in the dazzling ways of fairies, elementals who sparkle nature with light. They bless as they fly with glittering antennae, wave golden wands, or leave streams of diamond light in their path. You may not take these beings seriously, but I believe in the skill of fairy ministrations that exhibit magical powers! We can resonate with their ideals and actions. We think of the magical characters of Tinker Bell and the Fairy Godmother in Cinderella. Their sparkling is positively enchanting! The Fairy Godmother was so impressive that, when she waved her wand, she conjured magical shoes, a magnificent gown, and a glorious carriage with coachmen for Cinderella to attend the ball. My dream is to have this skill of total sparkling manifestation, just once, for the amazement, joy, happiness and life change that it could bring! She inspired me to act as a fairy godmother to several children for whom I play this special role. One of these extraordinary children lovingly made me a sparkling wand with special gemstones, which I treasure. I always use it in her presence to her delight!

These fairy tales and magical stories appeal to all ages, but especially to young children, who are easily in touch with fairies and angels, and who reveal a high quality of consciousness and playfulness. They both bring goodness to life, often through miraculous means. Children pretend to be princesses and fairy creatures in their make-believe play who freely wave their wands for magical happenings and surprising results. I believe that this unique form of expression makes children feel beautiful, special, and empowered. As pure hearts, they also want to share their shining, innocent light with others. It makes us feel happy to watch them. Sparkle to enliven the joy of your inner Divine child with or without a wand.

Sparkling inspiration can come from anywhere and may be right outside your front door! Even a spider can inspire you. When I was writing my doctoral dissertation, a large spider arrived one day on an eave of my porch. He had such a presence and wove such a beautiful glistening web that I could not brush him away. He reminded me of a character called Haunchy the Spider, in one of my early favorite children's books, *Little Squeegy Bug, Story of a Firefly*, by Bill and Bernard Martin. Haunchy Spider wove an intricate pair of beautiful silver wings for his friend, Squeegy, who wanted to fly to the moon and stars to become "Lamplighter of the Skies." The spider on my porch turned out to be a true sparkler and power animal to me. He became my daily companion and my most inspirational writing guide. He proceeded to weave stronger versions of his translucent, mandala-like web, which looked like a grid of luminous gems. He reflected to me my own brilliance, artistic gifts, steady work ethic, and wholeness. His threads marvelously caught differing light hues throughout the day and night. It honestly felt like my consciousness was linked to a portal of light, carrying wisdom from beyond the stars.

This spider and his web stayed with me for over a year. We were in resonance. The day that I successfully defended my dissertation, I came home to excitedly tell my spider what we had accomplished together as co-creators. Poof! He and the web were gone...just like Mary Poppins! The presence and perfect timing of this unexpected muse moved me deeply. He changed my entire perspective on the possibilities of life's profound mysteries, with so many synchronicities. The process of metamorphosis is amazing, when tiny acorns grow to become a mighty tree, or when a squiggly caterpillar transforms into a beautiful butterfly. In the same way, the art of sparkling has transformed me to grow by leaps and bounds. My growing capabilities are weaving a new form of my physical and energetic being. I have noticed my psychological and spiritual growth. You witness yourself, morphing from a regular human into a divine human being. You can literally dance and sparkle in light and empower others in miraculous ways.

Your dreams may inspire your sparkling! Another unlikely group of animals showed up in a dream the week before I decided to write this book. I dreamt that there was a pile of ten gray-brown platypuses right outside my door. They were relaxing in the sun on the front porch. What were they trying to communicate to me? The dream gnawed at me and I felt deeply curious about this strange message coming from my higher self. I studied up about the platypus, who looks more unusual than I had imagined, with a large bill and funny, webbed feet. They are mammals called monotremes, who lay eggs and who are the last remaining representatives of their genus, which has survived for millions and millions of years on our planet earth.

How does this relate to sparkling? Do you know that platypuses are the only land animals in the world that have a sixth-sense sonar system? Their large bill has thousands of cells that both generate electrical impulses and detect the electrical fields of living things through a process called electrolocation. Their eyes, nose and mouths are closed as they hunt, but they locate their food in the water by sensing electrical currents. They apparently represent an ancient breed of sparklers! They arrived in my dream as divine messengers to bring me their collective wisdom and to support me in the writing of this book. This moved me to empower my readers with this new art of sparkling for the empowerment of both humans on earth.

This dream also allowed me to fully embrace my own energetic abilities and peculiarities. Do you have hidden traits you fear to own? Don't be afraid to confront your own resistances. As an academic college professor, I was not keen to write a book about sparkling. Then I realized that you must appreciate all your gifts, which may seem odd to others. Don't be afraid to be who you truly are in all your unique expressions. My hybrid skillset created sparkling in the first place. My special contribution is to pass on this new form to you. It appears to be the right time to share and expand the use of these transformative sparkling abilities.

Look for your sparkling catalysts awake and asleep who may come your way! Inspiration may come from holy teachers, enduring symbols, dazzling fairies, creatures, characters in books, real life power animals and from within your own psyche. Who or what has motivated you to live a life of greatness? Importantly, take big steps to keep growing and evolving to become your own best spiritual inspiration. The goal of the most enlightened spiritual masters is for each of us to discover our own light and love which we bring in to play. Power up to claim and live the fullness of your Divine inheritance. Become further enlightened by listening to your soul and embodying the array of many wisdom teachings from these sparkling presences and inspirational teachers!

We are all manifestations of oneness, vibrating at different levels of consciousness and frequencies. Join with this radiant family to uplift all of us and serve mankind by weaving light strands for peace, hope, and new visions for the world.

> *"We have only to remember that Nature's 'magic wand' need not be an external force, but an internal desire coupled with an extraordinary opinion about our greatness and the inevitability of the steps we are about to take to achieve that aim."*
>
> — *Jacob Needleman, A Sense of the Cosmos*

My Sparkling Teachers

*"Let's explore the wavelength that seems to
distinguish people whose highest aspirations
appear to bloom in the world."*

—— Jean Houston

THIS BOOK IS ABOUT THE LIGHT within all of us and how to use it
to sparkle life. The origin of my sparkling comes from a time
just after my birth. I honestly remember experiencing deep
contact with two tall angels who lovingly appeared to me in
a tower of expansive light over my crib. These angels were
my very first teachers. They told me the greatest truth about
myself: "Go forth. Be the light." This holy, timeless encounter
left a clear imprint in my heart and soul. These angels gave me
my soul mission to bring more light into the world, but I was
too little to understand this inspiring message. It was years
before I clearly understood what to do. Mark Twain said,
"The two most important days in your life are the day you are
born and the day you find out why."

When I was still young, it was very important to me to
dress as a firefly for my first Halloween at school. My favorite

book at the time, *Little Squeegy Bug,* was about a firefly who had a lantern in his tail who lit up the skies for his friends. My costume had an actual light in the tail, which I could turn on with a small remote control. I felt so proud in kindergarten during the school parade to shine my light for other children's happiness. My five-year-old self would be so proud to know that I have become a real "sparkler" in my later years, teaching others how to do this. Trust your early instincts and passions, which may reveal your life's plan. *Remember who you are, what you are here to do, and who inspired you.*

During my personal journey, I received tremendous knowledge from teachers who were trailblazers in their fields, who motivated me to fully uncover my talents. My father motivated me early on to stay positive, love learning, and to look for the best teachers in my chosen area of study. What great advice this turned out to be! These brilliant teachers left an indelible mark on my soul to polish its golden gleam, as great teachers do. I became a pioneer in two new fields: dance-movement therapy and prenatal and perinatal psychology. My teachers gave me many keys that finally opened the main lock that revealed the art and science of sparkling to me. They came at regular intervals and each one brought me a different piece of knowledge. Upon reflection, meeting each one seems mysteriously orchestrated to present the next perfect nugget of wisdom, until I could put all the pieces of the puzzle together. They inspired me to discover my own innate gifts and spiritual unfolding. These teachings, unbeknownst to me at the time, percolated to fuel the greater fulfillment of my soul mission.

When you are ready, the perfect teacher finds you. I am deeply grateful to my beautiful teachers! All carried the blazing torch of wisdom. Looking back, all my best teachers sparkled with light. When I was in their presence,

I felt empowered by their vibratory intelligence of Wisdom and Truth. Great teachers give you more than theoretical or spiritual understandings. You may get goosebumps and or electrical pulses in your body. When you hear the Truth being spoken, your inner divine sparkler may activate. This process has inspired me to evolve, pass down their work, and teach my own truth to my students. As we are all one in spirit, everything I have learned applies directly to you, and is not about me. Perhaps you can consider how your own life is being informed and inspired. We stand on the shoulders of our elders, mentors and teachers however we meet them, and it is important to honor them. Now I am thrilled to introduce you to some of my best ones.

MY GRANDMOTHER: SPARKLING LOVE

My grandmother's radiance sparkled! What a great gift it was for me to live with my maternal grandmother, Kathryn Brittain Myers, during my early formative years, between the ages of one and four, when my mother was too ill to take care of me. A tragedy turned into a blessing. My grandmother impressed upon me her daily, lighthearted goodness and kindness. Her living messages inspire me to this day.

She truly loved caring for me, and she consciously exposed me to artistic, literary and spiritual refinement. We laughed all the time. She lit up my world and encouraged me to dance, sing, and play to my heart's content. She sparkled my life and the lives of others. She wrote messages to herself about how to be a good person and kept them in her Bible, which I still have. She played Chopin frequently, which deeply moved my three-year-old heart. I danced passionately with a flowing light-heartedness as she played the piano. Many times, I danced on top of her coffee table as I felt carried away to improvise with abandon. I came down the stairs each morning hearing her play music. We loved to sing many kinds of songs from her old sheet music, including Christmas music that we sang together all year round. She read fine literature and poetry to me out loud, which captured my vivid imagination into adolescence.

Before I went to bed each evening, my grandmother used the healing power of words and touch. Often, she recited poetry.

> Our Lady of the Twilight,
> She hath such gentle hands,
> So lovely are the gifts she brings
> From out of sunset lands.
> — Alfred Noyes

She always gently massaged my face and rubbed my back and legs. Her complete nurturing soothed all my cares and allowed me to fall asleep peacefully. I have always included loving touch in my nighttime rituals to soothe my children and grandchildren. Like her, I use my hands as a form of energetic expression to share my love.

My grandmother was a guiding star who showed me how to brighten and transform life by using my hands in creative ways. She planted many kinds of flowers in her garden and we dug in lots of dirt. She arranged flowers that won ribbons at the Adair County Fair in Kirksville, Missouri. Each week, she made and brought bouquets of flowers to cheer up sick friends and elderly people. She created beautiful table arrangements each day to bring beauty to my grandfather, who returned home deaf from the war.

One of my favorite memories was watching her make bread from scratch with her strong hands. This simple gesture of continuously and repetitively sifting the flour into the dough left a lasting visceral impression that has inspired my sparkling technique. She literally sparkled the food as she prepared it. I can still recall the smell of baking bread and the taste of her food. These memories fill me with such joy and have inspired my gift of spontaneously spreading sparkle blessings.

All your life, you remember special moments from childhood. We can deeply affect and influence others' lives by holding a sparkling nature, just being ourselves. My grandmother taught me the power of love, tenderness, graciousness and beauty. She encouraged me to passionately love what I do and to bless and to sparkle life with all my heart in everyday life.

I have tried to pass down her sparkling and caring ways to my children and grandchildren. I was directly inspired by her daily focus on God, tireless dedication to friends and community, aesthetic perspective, love of literature, and the many ways that she created meaning and beautiful moments.

What lights up your heart and makes your being sparkle? Who has inspired you to love, feel good and embody your greatness? How do you sparkle in life? Because we are all connected, your simple sparkling can touch the world. Create beautiful moments that express love and beauty and send out your light with sparkling moments that create goodness!

GENE KELLY: SPARKLING FLOW

During my junior year in college, I decided to study at the UCLA Dance Department for a semester. Choreography was my favorite class. One day, our teacher, Penny Lewitt, told us that a surprise teacher was coming to our class.

It was Gene Kelly, the consummate dancer and movie star, known for his innovative contributions that combined dance and film. When he came to our class, he wanted to select dancers interested in choreography for a professional dance project. Kelly was the embodiment of the ultimate celestial dance master. He exhibited the vitality, majesty and strength of a fluid, emotive, human body in glorious motion. He was in his mid-fifties by then, but he radiated the youth of a man half his age with an incredibly fit and athletic body. I loved him at first sight!

His charming smile and personality radiated megawatt warmth with 100 percent Sparkle Star Power! His sparkling essence was totally embodied. He selected me and four others to dance his choreography. I was overwhelmed with shock, bliss and joy! We worked with him for four or five days for a short-term professional engagement.

We all wondered why he wanted UCLA dancers and not more-professionally trained and experienced ones. He told us he wanted to work with performers who would not just do the steps by rote, but who would bring intelligence, heart, zing, creativity and meaning to the performance. I learned more from him that week than perhaps from any other dance performer or teacher. It was a time of hard work of course. From what I have read about him later, I know that he had mellowed a lot from once being a difficult taskmaster. Kelly offered us a much less arduous teaching approach, than when he had first taught Debbie Reynolds to dance at nineteen. I was her same age and thankfully, had a very different experience than she.

Kelly taught us that our own movement flow could effortlessly glide with total smoothness from our inner self without resistance. His dancing looked like he was floating on air. Such lightheartedness came from his heart too. We took away a sense of mastery that felt elegant and elevated that we could later apply to our life. I try to share the unforgettable joy of his smile.

As dancers in training, most of our other teachers had pushed us physically to the limit. They wanted the best leap through arduous training. I was forcing my dancing and trying to be perfect. Traditional dance techniques stressed our bodies and muscles, which was painful. Personally, I tried so hard to be a good dancer that my dancing looked strained and had lost its fun.

Gene Kelly taught us a very different approach. It was all about the total joy of dancing while entering its flow. All great athletes enter flow states. Kelly quintessentially embodied and taught a surrender to the dance itself. You can immediately see this in his hypnotic film performances. He inspired us to move with pure ease from the beginning. He did not want us to copy his movements as he showed us the choreography but encouraged us to add our own creative sparkle to the mix.

We learned Kelly's choreography in a completely miraculous way. It felt like a sparkling transmission. Looking back, we worked with dedication and diligence that week as we learned the complex movement combinations. However, we did not practice piece-by-piece steps or movement sequences over and over. We became confident that all our movements would flow in the right order and manner, without a worry, and they did.

We literally knew that we could "sing and dance in the rain" like he had done. It felt like we were accessing multiple dimensional points of brilliance that were available to us with each step. Somehow, he got all of us into a group bliss state of high consciousness, in which anything was possible.

I cellularly experienced harmony in my body, without any feeling of separation. As Richard Rudd wrote in *Gene Keys*: "The higher subtle bodies of humankind are designed to self-organize into potent and coherent formations of awakened beings." In our performance, everything we communicated appeared fresh and flowed gracefully from start to finish, which felt like heaven on earth. From that moment on, we embodied the flow of our beloved teacher.

What are the lessons from my experience with such a talented dancer and passionate and dedicated artist? Kelly restored to me the love of dance that my sweet soul had passionately expressed while dancing on top of my grandmother's coffee table at four years of age. My exuberance for dance was rejuvenated that week and has never left my body or soul.

I stopped pushing my body to its limits. I have not talked much about my one week dancing experience with Kelly, as it felt just too unreal and magical. I did not want to diminish this sacred and blissful encounter and did not really know how to incorporate it into my life when I later decided not to become a professional dancer or choreographer. However, I want to share the positive elements of Kelly's teaching that have greatly empowered my sparkling abilities.

Gene Kelly gave me two incredible gifts: the spirit of exhilaration and the love of daily movement flow. He transmitted full sparkle power to us, his dancers, that filled our audience with great warmth and happiness during each performance. "Gotta dance" was Kelly's mantra and mine is… "gotta sparkle!"

Sparkling is a state of heart and mind whose spirit enters the body. You can radiate with sparkling energies like Kelly did! How often are we ever encouraged to emit bright cellular glow in daily life? Make this a habit that you cultivate. Express more lightness of being that emanates from you without any strain. There is never any forcing in your sparkling. This simple act makes you and others feel relaxed and happy. Express joy when you genuinely feel it. This sublime feeling is beneficial to others, who share your company as they receive the radiance of your light.

Do not underestimate the power of a smile, contagious exuberance and the power to be moved by an artistic or musical performance. You can dance in life without being a great dancer! The key is to keep an upbeat attitude, stay moving, and practice walking in flow. Flow connects you with all eternal talents and capabilities. I believe that every great artist, athlete and successful entrepreneur taps into this state from the passion of what they are doing.

Leap into the unknown, enter its timeless flow and move unleashed to the place where creation begins. You are lifted into the magic of every quantum moment. Enjoy the thrill too of living as energetic, moving beings of light who literally dance on magical currents of wave particle of light every day! I am moved to sparkle as I dance in flow anywhere upon the wings of love. I grin broadly and imagine Gene Kelly as my inspiring companion on my sparkling jaunts. Ask him to join you, and he just might!

MARY STARKS WHITEHOUSE: SPARKLING AUTHENTIC ESSENCE

Mary Starks Whitehouse, one of my most invaluable teachers. She was both a pioneer in dance-movement therapy and her own movement improvisational process. She was the founder of authentic movement, a non-verbal, improvisational movement practice that was first called "movement in depth." I have facilitated authentic movement for more than forty years. She blew my mind in a movement workshop at Hampshire College. I was a psychology and dance double major at Mount Holyoke College and was participating in a leadership workshop. I had been chosen as the only student representative, among other participating heads of the fine arts departments, to design the five-college dance consortium for the colleges of Mount Holyoke, Smith, Amherst, Hampshire and the University of Massachusetts Amherst.

Whitehouse came from California to direct movement facilitation for this group. We were spearheading an innovative new program that pooled resources from these campuses to benefit student majors in an inter-campus collaborative effort. Much to my delight, this program is still wildly flourishing many years later, offering some of the best dance studies in the country.

It was uncomfortable being the only young female student dancer among brilliant, awkward, adult men. I danced full on, improvising creatively in the group. Then Whitehouse tapped me on the shoulder and quietly said: "Go to the corner of the room and lie down until you are moved." I was completely deflated but followed her instructions.

I lay there waiting impatiently for a long time with nothing happening, until I noticed my breath was rising and falling. There was some tension release as my body sunk into the floor with relaxation. Then out of the blue...a slow movement flow arose from nowhere, moving my right arm from the stillness of my soul. I *was moved*. This unexpected movement reflected a very different self-expression, which was quite fluid. This felt authentically me, because I was listening and responding organically to my own inner intuitive impulses, rather than consciously directing my own dance experience. This experience was a liberating moment of pure being that I shall never forget.

That moment I surrendered to a slower movement flow that just unfolded naturally to make a deeply authentic gesture from my soul. My true self felt like an eternal flame that had its own natural motion that I did not have to force. This was a new beginning with so many dimensions, which would lift me out of a box. Years later, my core knowing would move in the direction of sparkling, which happens through spontaneous movement flow.

During my adolescence I never stopped being active long enough to just rest and let go of busy distractions. I was only twenty-one then but had made myself a nervous wreck from academic pressures that had given me an ulcer. Intellectual pursuits in high school and college had been my primary lens, with a focus on using my logical brain only.

This initial unwinding experience was the catalyst for my clear knowing that I no longer had to push against myself to accomplish my goals. Also, I realized the possibility that a future dance career could be a vehicle for growth and healing arts and not solely about performance art. I had to explore my own inner contemplative movement, whose practice moves you to experience your authentic self and express its depth, along with that of your soul.

That four-hour experiential workshop with Mary Whitehouse changed my life's direction and career trajectory. Instead of studying clinical psychology, I pursued graduate studies in dance therapy at UCLA and studied authentic movement in depth. Later, I became an artist of soul-making as an authentic movement practitioner/dance therapist and then a psychologist. The order of this unfolding was perfect.

It's wonderful to take the time to explore other parts of yourself, which leads you to your wholeness. Just allow something new to organically unfold in your life, according to its own timing. This takes a level of trust that is best not to judge. Your intuitive knowing can help you to effortlessly guide your future steps in personal and professional areas. One moment of expanded awareness can bring clarity that enlarges your perceptions, bringing new perspectives about yourself and your life.

Mary Whitehouse opened the doors to access my body wisdom, soul and my greater transcendent sparkling being. I have experienced her authentic movement process in great depth over several decades and have become a movement facilitator of this practice for more than forty years.

In authentic movement, there are usually two participants. The "mover" who experiences the process of authentic movement and the "witness" who observes the mover with no judgment. In both roles, you notice the movement of constantly shifting energy, feelings, and expressions of being. It is also facilitated in groups. There is always something new to learn about yourself. It is about liberating yourself to express your authentic feelings, while you are held in a safe container by the witness.

Mary Whitehouse and her process awakened me to personal growth that elevated my consciousness and took me on a grand, life-changing adventure! She gave me ways to play with a wealth of new observations and abilities that eventually led me on my journey to become a sparkler.

Sparkling engages your mind only to clarify your intent. It relies on you to contact your heart intelligence with its vast knowing. You are a unique expression of a greater Oneness that allows you to shine with magnitudes of light. When I sparkle light, I feel expanded, moving from the stillness and depth of my soul: As a sparkler, you simultaneously participate as a mover of energies and stay in a witness mode.

When you simply relax and take a big breath, like I did on that spring day in 1970, you allow yourself to just be in the present moment, which can take you home to discover your own real authentic self. Early and adult programming can influence you to stay in your egoic self. This can take you away from the true expression of your original essence. Uncover and remove any superficial layers. Find your way back to that authentic place inside of you that simply reveals the pure expression of the sparkling light that you are.

ESALEN INSTITUTE: *SPARKLING HUMAN POTENTIAL AND NATURE*

In the early seventies, while completing my master's degree in dance/dance therapy at UCLA, I was deeply fortunate to spend a lot of time at Esalen Institute in Big Sur, California. This is always my forever soul place; it exudes indescribable beauty against the backdrop of the sparkling radiance of the Pacific Ocean.

Esalen at that time was the center of the human potential movement and I was there in its heyday. My college boyfriend lived and worked there. He was studying with Ida Rolf, the founder of Structural Integration, to become a Rolfing practitioner. Many great souls who were thought leaders from various fields of study visited regularly to teach in this New Age community.

It was an honor to take workshops with Joseph Campbell, the mythologist; Alan Watts, the philosopher who popularized Eastern teachings; Al Huang, the tai chi master; and George Leonard, the writer and educator. We did many kinds of creative and spiritual exercises, like experiential mirroring, holographic breathing, and rebirthing.

I also did intense encounter groups with Fritz Perls, the founder of Gestalt therapy, and Julian Silverman, a clinical psychologist. The focus was on developing the light of our awareness and on being authentic in the moment. We acted out our dreams and shadow parts of ourselves. We used movement and vocal exercises as primal expressions to avoid "head-tripping."

Personal and group breakthroughs in human potential were made at Esalen. It was both an incredible environment and atmosphere of enlightened people and ideas that mattered. For the first time in my life, I felt truly alive, relaxed, beautiful, and free to be myself, without influence of family and other societal pressures.

The exhilarating frequencies of Big Sur filled me with so much vitality that my spirit soared to a state of transcendence. I was always "high" there, but not on pot or other drugs. Exposure to all these visionaries and their inspired teachings brought me sparkling cosmic joy!

I entered many altered states of consciousness doing ecstatic dance around the fires led by Gabrielle Roth, who later developed the Five Rhythms. She often stated, "In trance we move into the bigger picture." We surrendered our more formal selves to dance with primitive, tribal movements.

Though I was a dancer, these undulating rhythms had never been in my movement repertoire. I learned many transformative practices that focused on body awareness and internal feelings and senses, with emphasis on full body breathing and sensory awareness. Through this experiential work, my body felt like a portal accessing heaven and earth that could receive internal messages from my intuition, heart and higher self. Through this gateway, I was gaining access to cellular memories stored in my preconscious and subconscious, that connected me to my bodily wisdom.

My psychic abilities were also developing through the dynamic alchemy of these interconnections. I became fully embodied in Big Sur. My experiences there were all out of the ordinary for me, based upon my Midwest conservative background, yet it all felt so comfortable and natural.

These experiential sessions supplemented my academic learning in dance-movement therapy and allowed me to feel good and to move forward confidently in my field of study. One memorable afternoon, I scheduled an appointment with the resident astrologer, who lived in a geodesic dome on the grounds. He was highly recommended by everyone there. He did my astrological chart and told me that my life's career focus would be on examining and discovering the art and science of my professions. His prediction, which sounded astounding to a twenty-one year-old, turned out to be entirely correct, as my future would be spent gathering conceptual foundations for all my fields, including sparkling. Pass along your gifts in the manner that is unique to you.

Take the time to have many adventures in your life that inform you. You learn so much about yourself that you do not normally learn in school. My early Esalen experience exposed me to free spirits, expressive souls, intellectuals, and bodyworkers so different from my parents, teachers and friends. I discovered my potential there and realized later that I was just like them, as they were my tribe. My future careers would all incorporate expressive arts, based in body experiencing. Pass along your gifts in the manner that is unique to you.

While dancing in the canyons of Big Sur adjacent to the Esalen properties, I actually "followed my bliss," while expressively journaling, drumming, dancing and sparkling. This translated to me as flowing with the harmony of a virtually untouched and hidden area in nature and filling up with the power from the elemental forces inhabiting this special area.

In this holy place of deepest silence, I danced with abandon among huge verdant ferns, stony surfaces, rocks with lichen, and magnificent redwood trees pulsing with living radiance. My essential lightness of spirit from childhood returned with the freedom of movement to explore this otherworld.

Nature's wildest places touch my soul very deeply because I commune with their palpable energetic vibrancy, which brings me a feeling of strength. The Maoris and Hawaiians describe this as receiving mana or spiritual power. It is when you commune with rocks, stars, clouds, animals, trees and animals along with people...all sentient life that calls you home into the oneness.

At Esalen, I first spontaneously started to sparkle nature in pure states of awareness and joy *as I was moved*. My gift of sparkling playfully emerged in this special environment. The lush landscapes called me to join them in the dance of light as I fully appreciated their wondrous beauty.

The canyons were rather dark, but I could frequently see shafts of pure sunlight enter them with streams of sparkles that illuminated greenery to make it glow! Also, I felt the real presence of fairies living within the moss mounds of these magical glens. They felt to me as though they were sparkling life there and I joined right in the fun! At night, I would go up to the road and spontaneously sparkle the stars as they twinkled me back in sync. This seemed extraordinary to me. I felt that we were directly communicating with each other and that I could have a relationship with all sentient beings. What a magical and important time in my life! I was opening to new aspects of myself that I hadn't known existed and it felt very safe.

There I experienced the first emergence of myself as a natural woman, mystic, shaman, dancer, and sparkler. This captivating, rugged environment with pristine elements just naturally drew all of this out of me without any formal teaching. My essence loved feeling a flowing light dancer in both physical and energetic forms. I was free to play in real and virtual reality and explore new abilities to exist in two places or dimensions at the same time. For example, I could be sparkling on a star as well as doing normal activities somewhere back on earth. As an energetic being, I can travel with my consciousness to any location, like a big soaring bird, and let my imagination flow to send my sparkling energies wherever they are needed.

My shamanic skills were opening, which felt powerful. Everything was me. It felt like I could shapeshift and merge into other forms and fields. This was my first initiation into the mysteries of infinite possibilities and the highest frequencies of ecstasy and bliss. I felt completely tuned into all of it. I was one with the rhythms of Nature and moving in the flow of Her subtle energies. The more that I was attuned, the more refined my senses became. When reading this quote by the astrologer, Bill Attride, I deeply remembered my first Big Sur experience: "You are a sparkling field of energy forms who with innumerable others moves through luminous Fields of life and love that is One."

Practice your sparkling outdoors while appreciating nature around you. Being with natural beauty anywhere is inspiring and makes you feel such a spirit of gratitude and openness to life. You can relax and awaken all your senses as you return to the timeless present moment that may open the door to other realities. It is important to go back to special places in Nature that you have loved, where you have felt safe, at peace, and happy, and re-enter the natural flow of life again. You just know that magic happens there. My memories of the exquisite Big Sur terrain with rolling green hills, flowering lupines, the majestic beauty of the redwoods, and shimmering waters of the ocean are fully inscribed in my heart's core and stored for retrieval at any time.

Use any captivating memories as an energetic resource to stir up more good feelings when you are feeling low or depleted. Remembering life-giving moments that hold happy magical vibrations can immediately raise your frequencies and further animate your sparkling abilities anytime.

Because Big Sur is so special to me, I have visited it many times in my life to recharge and deeply commune with my fullest self. Big Sur always fills me with high vibrational magical sparkles and energies that directly access the knowing of my wise soul. My first memory of sparkling happened there along ago.

Yet, it was not until years later that I spontaneously sparkled once more in my husband's office, and then began to explore the practice with real depth as an energetic form. How important it is to spend your time creating extraordinary moments, whose memory sustains you throughout your life.

My sparkling is infused with the magical energies and new age consciousness of my first extraordinary Esalen and Big Sur experience. This year-long period awakened my potentials, offering profound gifts of power, awe and wonder. Sparkle to just let go, play, offer praise, and surrender to the present moment every day, and enter the bliss as you take the time to open to the Infinite.

Valerie Hunt: sparkling biofields

In the early seventies, when I was pursuing my master's degree in dance movement therapy at UCLA, I received a paid scholarship to work with Dr. Valerie Hunt, who was professor emeritus of physiological sciences. I became her research assistant in her Movement Behavior Lab, which was later renamed the Bioenergy Research Laboratory.

Hunt was an extraordinary scientist and visionary who studied the existence of light frequencies surrounding all living things. Becoming exposed to Hunt's research changed my life early on and vastly benefited my professional career. It had huge implications for me as a person, dance therapist, mothering coach, and sparkler. I maintained personal contact with Hunt during her long, noteworthy scientific career into her nineties.

During my internship, she was investigating the aura around the leaf, in collaboration with Russian scientists, and studying the dynamics of early movement education. Later as a dance therapist, I developed movement programming for young children based on her research about the childhood origins of your daily movement behavior style.

Being with Hunt was an unforgettable daily adventure. As her research assistant, she had me write up her research in a scholarly way for articles and make time-consuming, creative drawings to illustrate the concepts. I now realize that she wanted me to access my two brain hemispheres to fully perceive and understand the fascinating content through different lenses of perception. What a remarkable start to my scientific education to become a *whole* brain thinker on the research topics of light and movement education. I sparkle from my right brain and whole brain, not from my left.

Hunt was the first American scientist to make the groundbreaking discovery that an aura surrounds your physical body. This aura is a broad-spectrum electromagnetic energy field that works like a prism to refract different wavelengths of light.

According to people who are psychically able to "see" the aura, it radiates with a corona-like shape around the outside of the body: "The pool of electromagnetic energy around an object or person allows energy exchange. This corona, invisible to most people, is seen at times as a halo or light-colored mist around a living body," Hunt wrote in her book, *Infinite Mind*.

The aura's major functions are to be in continuous exchange with the environment and to receive vital, ever-changing information about all the energies from objects, people and places in our energetic field. It shines brightly when the individual is healthy.

Hunt's innovative research scientifically confirmed that the aura could be measured and graphically shown using her new technology, which she called an Aura Meter. This instrument made invisible frequencies of subtle energies visible, and NASA scientists later refined its design. It could detect and measure a thousand times more electrical activity in the body than any other scientific equipment. The aura is the body's fastest electrical system, continuously changing its patterning, oscillating up to one million cycles per second.

As her research progressed over decades, it became clear that the human energy field/aura is comprised of not just one layer, but seven different layers of subtle or energy bodies that she called biofields. They surround the physical body like a series of nesting eggs. Each layer holds different colors, higher functions and electromagnetic frequencies that, together, reveal comprehensive information about you.

There are three bodies on the physical plane, three on the spiritual plane, and the astral body that bridges the physical and spiritual planes. The etheric body is the densest layer, closest to the physical body. Next is the emotional body, then the mental body, astral body, etheric template, celestial body, and causal body.

Her discoveries confirmed that disease can be first seen and measured in the first layer of the human biofield, before it enters the physical body. This means that disease can be treated before it manifests in the physical body. Early discovery of a potential illness in the biofield can prevent the occurrence of some disease. Hunt stated that if you correct the disturbance in the field, then your symptoms go away. As technologies improve, perhaps this type of diagnostic scanning will someday be made available to predict and diagnose disease.

Hunt emphasized that a healthy, strong, and stable energy field exhibits a wide range of frequencies. A healthy aura is well organized and not chaotic. Hunt's research revealed that anticoherent or chaos patterns are caused by stress and are the root of disease.

It is important to be mindful of your exposure to discordant energies to maintain sparkling, healthy biofields. Hunt taught me to consider the conditions of biofields, as they can become weak or strong before you know it. Every thought and feeling changes the makeup of the energetic flux within the biofield. Your biofields reveal your electromagnetic chemical condition at any moment and register every inner state, thought, feeling, and hidden pattern as a subtle emanation.

Hunt discovered that "each person has his own unique signature field or pattern of frequencies, that functions as a base reference from which his field responds to other fields" (*Mind Mastery Meditations*).

The energetic frequencies of a person are both unique and continuous as "energy patterns and wave shapes." Also, the conditions and depths of experiences to which you are exposed continuously change your unique fields of light. It is paramount to be in touch with yourself on an energetic level.

A buildup of negative thoughts, feelings and old traumas can clog biofields, causing stagnation and poor energy flow. This looks like a gray or darkened film that is essentially like frozen light. With awareness and energetic tools, you can learn how to clear your aura fields of blockages and distortions from unhealthy attachments and subconscious programming. Your self-care should involve energetic clearing and the daily routine of raising your frequency. My sparkling practice does this for me.

Hunt discovered that a therapist or healer with a coherent, healthy field can change a client's anticoherent field to move into greater frequencies of health. People respond differently to their therapists/coaches/physicians, as well as to energetic practices and therapies.

It is important to discover which therapist or treatment is right for you. Trust your bodily intuition when you are choosing your medical and support people. Your body senses when a coherent field is compatible with yours for your best support and healing.

This research had implications for my professional career. I realized the quality of my own unique energy field could positively impact my clients' and family members' health and well-being. I became motivated to build greater energetic potency and coherency within myself, so I adopted the spiritual practices of authentic movement, meditation and, later, sparkling. My personal goal was to de-stress, raise my own frequency, stay heart-centered and engage with movement flow, in order to serve my clients and family in states of body-mind coherence.

The knowledge gained from Hunt inspired me to develop sparkling as my energetic practice to help keep auric fields luminous. My sparkle power has been enhanced by learning as much as possible about the human aura and its biofields. As Barbara Marciniak wrote in Bringers of the Dawn: "Live by the Aura of being. It is a high state."

Use sparkling as a useful tool and spiritual practice to both clear and to amplify your biofields to boost health. Sparkle yourself, including your own energetic fields, which connect to other ever-expanding fields of light and permeate each other. The energetic state of your own biofields in turn influences the fields of others.

Sparkling as a spiritual practice can increase the vibration of your auric fields and personal chakras, so that they vibrate faster to elevate your overall frequencies. Then your magnetic power expands to match your frequency so you can manifest what you desire. You can positively affect others and your environment to catalyze shifts in consciousness by raising your frequencies.

Hunt's scientific contributions are enormous. The science of human vibration allows us to scientifically know that we are infinite and exist as moving fields of light. Hunt's remarkable research also helped lay the conceptual foundation for the emerging field of energy or vibrational medicine, which utilizes an array of modalities, such as acupuncture, reiki, dance, music therapies, and dowsing.

Scientific researchers are currently looking at the phenomena of the complete human bioenergy system and researching the effects of biofield treatments. I consider sparkling to be an additional energetic enhancement approach that may gain more mainstream acceptance in the future. Future research on biofield therapies and energetic medicine may shed more light on the effects of sparkling.

JACK SCHWARTZ: SPARKLING MIND-BODY STATES

Another amazing master teacher, Jack Schwartz, entered my life in my late thirties. Schwartz, the director of Alethia Institute, is recognized as the first health educator who taught principles of body, mind and spirit integration.

What an enlightened man he was! He exhibited the most amazing healing powers and psychic abilities, developed from his experience of surviving in a concentration camp. His sparkling presence emitted Pure Love, Light and Goodness! To this day, I keep his picture close to my bed, because seeing his great smile makes me smile. The light of his being added to the wisdom of his teachings.

He taught me many priceless skills to amplify my own light. These included ways to meditate, change my brain-wave states, upshift my frequency, and enhance my emotional well-being. I learned how to move into higher wavelengths of happiness, joy, and abundance on cue.

Here is some classic Schwartz wisdom that applies to you, as a potential sparkler!

Live in a meditative state of appreciation 24/7.

Shine a clear forcefield of light from your third eye to everything. Practice upgrading the quality of this light.

Protect your fields by putting up a tube of light around your body to shield your energies first thing in the morning.

Breathe very slowly and deeply to enter lower brain wave states, reduce stress, lower blood pressure, and bring in more oxygen for improved energetic flow.

Boost your energy by placing your right hand on your lower back (the sacrum) and your left on your crown of your head. Hold for two to three minutes, then and reverse your hands.

Shine a light from your forehead and scan your interior body and its organs to promote internal awareness of your bodily systems.

Learn about how you feel when you enter different brain-wave states. Listen to sounds. tones and chants calibrated for these states.

Monitor the quality of your actions, thoughts, and words, which affect your energies to raise your vibrations.

Schwartz' gifts were remarkable. For several years, he was a subject in a research study led by Dr. Elmer and Alyce Green in the Voluntary Controls Program at the Menninger Clinic. The purpose of this inquiry, according to Elmer Green, Ph.D., was to "promote the development and understanding of the science of consciousness and make available the teaching of ancient wisdom traditions."

The Greens pioneered the field of clinical biofeedback and developed some of the first biofeedback equipment. Schwartz was their superstar, who displayed amazing voluntary controls of physiologic states. He could self-regulate his psycho-physiological processes, like some yogi masters, to consciously change his brain states.

Demonstrations that highlighted his abilities of "mind over matter" were dramatic. Schwartz could lie on a bed of long, sharp nails with no discomfort or scratches. He could stick a rusted knitting needle through his entire bicep and not bleed. He gave scientific researchers a whole body of knowledge about brain-wave states that promote body and emotional regulation.

By studying Schwartz, scientists learned about different brain-wave states and their approximate specific frequencies: beta (12-35 Hz), alpha (8-12 Hz), theta (4-8 Hz) and delta (0.5-3 Hz). They discovered details about the alpha brain state, which promotes physical healing in the body. Anyone can enter this wonderful state by relaxing and deep breathing to the count of five, to get out of the logical mind.

From age seven on, most of us spend our waking time in logical beta mind. Younger children are in in theta and alpha states, while babies and toddlers are in the lowest delta frequency. It is important for parents to learn to shift their brain waves to be able to enter their child's world for better attunement and communication. For example, parents can make these important shifts when they slow down to enjoy playing with their children.

From Schwartz, I learned about my own voluntary controls, which allow me to fluidly shift my brain-wave states to awaken my potentials and cultivate whole-brain thinking. I can dial into alpha to benefit health and healing, move down to a deeper state of theta to promote creative thinking, and go further down into a delta state to commune with babies and work as a shaman.

With practice, you can learn to control your brain-wave states. Listen to sounds and tones that entrain your brain to enter specific frequencies. Meditation and yoga are other ways to control your brain states. Learning these voluntary controls helps you become a master in the art of sparkling, which is best practiced in alpha and theta frequencies with joyous flow and creativity.

Schwartz could both see and read auras to accurately recount all aspects of a client's personal development in spiritual, physical, emotional and mental aspects. He knew what you were here to accomplish and why.

Amazingly, he read my past and future from my auric field! In a personal session, he told me that my life had been seriously impacted in utero because my mother was stressed during her pregnancy. This caused me to have chemical and nutritional deficiencies that impacted my highest developmental potential. Specifically, he said that I did not have the necessary prenatal amounts of copper to fully wire my brain and develop my physical body.

This was an interesting revelation, as I had never considered my earliest history. This session motivated me to think about helping babies to receive the best start in life. Two years later, I began my doctoral studies of prenatal and perinatal psychology. Let's all sparkle babies in the womb at this critical stage of development.

Schwartz taught me so much about myself, body-mind integration, and about learning voluntary controls that put you in specific brain states for creativity, healing, pain reduction, and happiness. His encouragement eventually led me to become a master in the art of sparkling.

Whatever you think or feel, both consciously and unconsciously, can directly affect the manifestation of your physical reality. "*Dream the impossible dream,*" from the musical "Man of La Mancha," was Schwartz's personal motto. It inspires us now to become a sparkling miracle in progress.

Constantly radiate light from your bodily presence, third eye, and imagination to envision what you desire, with a strong, sparkling intention. As you take time to check in with yourself, you become increasingly aware of how your level of consciousness, personal actions, thoughts and beliefs are either life affirming or self-limiting. You have the power to keep your light shining and growing in amplitude.

Schwartz exhibited so many unusual capabilities and extraordinary talents that he was a sparkling example of realization of inner truth for his students. He was perhaps one of the prototypes of the new divine human. He instilled determination in me to become my highest expression of self to serve others with dedication. You can make a huge difference in the lives of others, unto future generations.

BRUCE LIPTON: SPARKLING CELLS AND DNA

Bruce Lipton, Ph.D., a cellular biologist, researcher, author, theorist and evolutionist, spoke as a guest lecturer in my doctoral program in prenatal and perinatal psychology. The entire lecture room vibrated with Lipton's contagious enthusiasm and passionate energies as he shared his groundbreaking research.

He has developed new theories supporting the new biology, epigenetics and prenatal and perinatal psychology. His conceptual foundations are based on the new physics that supports all fields of study. Lipton taught us that we are energy beings living in an energetic environment! This essential scientific orientation supports sparkling as an energetic tool.

Traditional assumptions based on a Newtonian mechanical reality, with the mind-body split, are no longer viable. Much of Western medicine operates with these outdated medical models, which are not aligned with new scientific paradigms.

Lipton asserts that change is slow in this medical system because much of the research is paid for by the trillion-dollar pharmaceutical industry. Lipton adopted the view that "energy is a *more* efficient means of affecting matter than chemicals."

This scientific paradigm supports the expression of energy dynamics and consciousness to bring change for healing purposes. In his article, *Mind over Genes: The New Biology,* he states: "the new physics emphasizes energetics over materialism, substitutes holism for reductionism and recognizes uncertainty over determinism." The truth of Lipton's ideas resonates within my being as well, as I activate my desire to sparkle. I have lectured on Lipton's body of work in my college classes in somatic psychology.

Lipton is an original thinker who is internationally sought after as a scientific lecturer about the new field of epigenetics. He has singlehandedly shifted scientific thinking about the nature and functioning of our genes. His main concept is that the expression of genes is influenced by nurture, environmental factors and even perceptions of the environment, and not programmed and limited by the genes you inherit.

"We are not controlled by our genes," he has repeated over and over. Lipton's expansive views on epigenetics have so many implications for health, well-being and aging. In the future, we will know exactly how the structure of inherited genes in our DNA can be modified to express themselves under different conditions. We can consciously sparkle our cells, organs and DNA strands for optimal functioning and performance.

Lipton teaches that each living cell contains batteries of amazing electrical force. When each cell combines and cooperates with trillions of other living cells in our bodies, you become a sparkling, limitless, energetic, cellular powerhouse. These potentials can be influenced by your positive thoughts and beliefs to generate internal harmonic conditions that optimize your health and healing.

He also emphasizes that you can consciously learn how to access and respond to the multidimensional energies in the universe that actively influence you. How? Lipton says that when you tune into your own heart, with its large electromagnetic field, you can discern whether good or bad vibrations are present. This small act can turn your life around.

Awareness and discernment are very important skills that help you know whom or what to attract or avoid for better overall functioning. Your heart is the key as you feel what is right or not for you in the moment. As energetic beings, we can consciously connect to and sparkle our cells, organs and DNA strands for optimal functioning and performance.

You sparkle at the level of your own reality. Stay in contact with positive energies as much as possible, to raise your vibration to sparkle with great potency. Obviously, you do not want to put yourself in harm's way and you need to avoid overly negative conditions at all cost. Awareness is needed in all your endeavors.

Use your intuition and heart's knowing to discern when it is best to apply sparkling. The more that you clear your own emotional baggage and release your constricting limiting beliefs, the greater your own light-filled capacities. Hopefully, all sparklers can learn how to tune into their own energy frequencies and make good choices to send out their best vibrations to whomever or whatever they are sparkling.

Lipton has moved the discussion from feeling victimized by our genetic endowment to feeling empowered to consciously change our beliefs and circumstances. Because you have the power to access the wisdom and vitality held in your body, you can use it as a tool for transformation. Awakening to your own power of intention and consciousness lights the path to improve your health and well-being. Your empowered will and desire for change stirs your own brain and body's circuitries to fulfill all latent potentials.

In his book, *The Power of Belief*, Lipton states, "Our new understanding of the Universe's mechanics shows us how the physical body can be affected by the immaterial mind. Thoughts, the mind's energy, directly influence how the physical brain controls the body's physiology."

New scientific foundations support sparkling as an effective energetic tool. It draws upon positive energies from the heart and mind to cooperatively imprint actions for beneficial outcomes that may be felt at the cellular level. As I write this book, I know that I will have to get in touch with my old teacher, who is the ultimate sparkling human being and who developed cutting-edge ideas for energetic medicine and its many applications. He would love sparkling!

Raymon Grace: Sparkling Healing Energies

In my early fifties I met Raymon Grace, a master dowser and teacher of dowsing. Dowsing is often used to locate water for farmers, but Grace primarily uses it as an energetic tool for health and healing. It is a skill that anyone can learn. He uses a pendulum, which looks like a small weight on a string, to yield miraculous results.

To dowse, you hold a clear intent to move energies for a positive outcome. You ask basic yes and no questions and twirl the pendulum to get answers. Then you can twirl it clockwise to increase positive energies or counterclockwise to clear negative or imbalanced energies. After any clearing, you then move the pendulum clockwise to fill up the void with positive energies.

Grace has been one of my most important teachers in life; he gave me a very simple, remarkable skill that I use daily to help my family and clients. Dowsing has so many applications. Sparkling is a similar resource that aligns you with your higher knowing and enhances and amplifies living energies but without using a pendulum.

Grace has been recognized as the number one healer in North America. There are few with his healing abilities anywhere, as he effortlessly cures many ailments with dowsing. He is the best person to have in your corner for immediate help.

My plain spoken, humble teacher is a mountain man who wears a cowboy hat and gun and lives in the hills of Virginia. He trained with Rolling Thunder and Chief Two Trees, who were both Cherokee healers, and studied with Jason Silva. Grace has been an invaluable mentor who has greatly furthered my energetic skills for almost twenty years. My dowsing and sparkling are indispensable to my life, and both are great skills to learn.

I first met Grace at a workshop he was leading. The day before, I had been shockingly diagnosed with uterine cancer, but decided to attend anyway. Afterward, I asked Grace if I had cancer. He twirled his pendulum and said, "Yep, you do!" Then he quickly moved his hands over my pelvic area and appeared to take something out. Next, he said, "Now you don't. It's gone."

Sure enough, he was correct. When I was re-examined and X-rayed in the following weeks, there was thankfully no cancer. This personal miracle strongly motivated me to become his student and learn his energetic techniques over the years. He writes about the basics in a small manual called *Techniques that Work for Me*. He frequently tells his students that everything is energy and that your thought follows energy. You can clear, manage and or move energies to remove probabilities that circumstances will happen in the future.

He emphasizes in his workshops the great importance of raising personal frequency for health purposes. Dowsing connects you to your Higher Self, who already knows the correct answer to the many questions you may ask.

Grace has established The Raymon Grace Foundation and is committed to several causes, including cleaning up our polluted waters in rivers, streams and oceans and replacing them with clean water. His cleared water tastes so much better than ordinary water. He believes that water easily picks up and holds nonbeneficial memories, even in your body, that need to be removed.

He has measurably reduced the rates of violence in communities and schools, lowered the incidence of sex trafficking in various countries, and cleared schools. He asks other dowsers to collectively commit to these agendas to improve conditions on the earth. His primary altruistic philosophy is that you don't know you can't do something unless you try. I also apply this philosophy all the time. Grace has taught me that small acts of kindness are never wasted.

Grace has many wonderful ideas for working with energy to improve your life. He taught me how to put up what he calls "energy cells" in all corners of my rooms. These are concentrated clusters that emit high frequency energies to improve overall health and well-being. I swing my pendulum clockwise to set them in place, supported by my clear intentions. That is all you need to do to create each powerful energetic vortex.

When my husband was recovering from a serious illness, I set these energy centers in the corners of his hospital room to promote his healing. When I work in hospitals and treatment centers as a therapist, I make a point to set these up, as the energies can quickly become stale, filled with lower frequency vibrations from emotional discharge.

I also sparkle the treatment rooms before I facilitate any therapeutic groups. The energetic difference that the energy centers and sparkling make is often noticed by the staff and patients, as the energy feels lighter and better in those rooms. You must discover ways to raise the frequencies of your environments. Avoid places with lowered vibrations or raise their vibrations through dowsing or sparkling.

Grace's energy work on me through the years has also allowed me to make shifts in my consciousness to embody higher frequencies. According to Lisa "Transcendence" Brown, in her book, *Navigating Dimensions*, "I may look the same, but the light particles within me are constantly being restructured to create a lighter version of me. The higher you vibrate, the faster you spin, the easier it is to move from realm to realm within."

I realize that apparent realities are not solid, but energetically flexible and capable of being reshaped! You can buy a pendulum, take online workshops with Grace, or meet him in a live workshop. My work with him has moved me to introduce sparkling as my own form of energy work. My approach does not focus on healing or make healing claims but exists to broadcast life-enhancing light for beauty, brilliance, replenishment, love, magic, and gratitude for life enhancement.

WENDY ANNE MCCARTY: SPARKLING BABIES

In 2000, I entered the first doctoral program in the country in the new field of prenatal and perinatal psychology at Santa Barbara Graduate Institute. This field provides education and psychological intervention to support babies through the earliest stages of life, from preconception, conception, pregnancy, birth, and early infancy into the first year. The field focuses on the baby's perspective because their earliest experiences set in motion core life patterns. These may be either life-enhancing or diminishing experiences that generate internal beliefs and imprints that affect later psychological perspectives for life, learning and relationships.

Wendy Anne McCarty, Ph.D., R.N., was the co-founding chair, with Marti Glenn, Ph.D., of my innovative doctoral program. A former obstetrical nurse, she was also a practicing prenatal and birth therapist, and a marriage and family therapist. McCarty inspired me to understand the remarkable consciousness of babies in the womb, at birth and during the first year of life. As David Chamberlain, one of the founders of prenatal and perinatal psychology, often said in his talks, "Babies appear to know more than they ought to know!"

In her booklet, *Being with Babies*, McCarty states: "What we are learning is revolutionizing the fundamental beliefs we have about prenates and babies and our ways of being with babies to support them." She encourages new parents, caregivers, and practitioners to attune to the baby's perspective and feelings, and to appreciate their sentient, sensitive nature.

Babies communicate non-verbally through facial expressions, eye contact, body language, postures, gestures, movement patterning, babbling, and crying, energetically and telepathically. These messages offer a well-spring of untapped knowledge and can tell us about their lives, earliest histories, and about our relationship dynamics with them. When we listen to their non-verbal communications and tune into their expressive, profound communications, we build mutual security, trust and understanding.

In McCarty's class, I learned that we are quantum, sentient beings with remarkable abilities that can go unrecognized and underdeveloped. This helped me understand a baby's perspective and transcendent nature. McCarty emphasized that the strong influence of the old Newtonian view in science had assumed we were just physical beings whose capacity for conscious awareness and abilities were based only on the brain and physical body's development. This limiting perspective did not leave room for us to acknowledge the expanded states and multidimensional abilities of babies.

In fact, new quantum paradigms are revealing that we are energetic, spiritual beings living in physical form. When a baby experiences nurturing conditions for their whole multidimensional being, they connect to their own primary transcendent consciousness so they can trust in their own knowing while in their human body. In addition, psychological nurture provided by parents and caregivers allows them to form positive beliefs and self-concepts that will extend to having good relationships in the future. This also builds the early brain and nervous system.

McCarty's book, *Welcoming Consciousness: Supporting Babies' Wholeness from the Beginning of Life* (2012), presents a groundbreaking multidimensional integrated model for infant development that incorporates prenatal and perinatal psychology and integral psychology with consciousness-based studies, early development, and energy psychology. Her main theoretical viewpoint is that babies begin life with an *integrated self*. Babies have dual awareness that includes both transcendent and human perspectives.

McCarty postulates that as babies are conceived and develop in the womb, their experiences are multidimensional. They carry capacities of knowing, awareness and perception, and are capable of intentional telepathic communication. They can consciously seek relationship with us from preconception forward. Her theory confirmed my earliest experience of interacting with the two angels who, after my birth, lovingly communicated my divine design and mission for this lifetime. I was telepathically aware of their communications to me.

By studying a baby's perspective of early experiences, prenatal and perinatal psychology-oriented therapies discovered how our lack of understanding and lack of caring for babies with their sentient nature in mind had detrimental outcomes with life-altering consequences. Even in the eighties we thought that babies undergoing surgery could feel no pain. Babies are sensitive, susceptible, and affected by myriad of experiences, such as not being wanted, toxic physical and emotional womb environments, medical birth interventions, and separation from their mother after birth. The earliest negative imprints, programming and trauma get stored in the subconscious mind to affect self-esteem.

I was negatively impacted into my adult life from the effects of early trauma with maternal separation for long periods. Releasing my early traumas received in the womb and after birth changed my life and nervous system and lowered my levels of anxiety.

I am honored to have been trained by McCarty, who taught that physical, emotional, mental, and energetic facilitation can assist in transforming and integrating difficult early experiences at all ages. These non-intrusive interventions can help resolve trauma and restore the individual at every level of their being.

She introduced me to energy psychology and encouraged me to receive other training to learn to use various energetic approaches that I have incorporated into my Mothering Coach practice and psychotherapy sessions. Working with these effective tools reinforced my desire to develop my sparkling method. Now I sparkle babies, pregnant women, and family members.

I have found that sparkling, as a subtle and gentle energetic modality, promotes health and happiness. It can offer great support and comfort to both mother and baby during the critical gestation period. I was moved to consistently sparkle my latest grandchild every day from pre-conception to birth. I witnessed the ease of the pregnancy and birth, which brought an exceptionally sparkling, alert, and healthy baby boy! Please try this out if you are a parent, grandparent, or friend.

We want all babies to receive the best sparkling start in life, following the principles of prenatal and perinatal psychology. Let us help them early on to stay connected to their inherent spiritual, transcendent selves throughout their lifelong journey. Sparkling is a gentle energetic tool that can be used by practitioners and parents to support and enhance babies' gifts of light-holding expanded spiritual abilities. Sending out light blesses and protects them when they are the most vulnerable in life. Let us keep all babies and children glowing and filled with radiant love and luminous light. They are quite energy sensitive and intuitively understand their innate powers from their enlightened nature. We must teach them in early childhood how to use their pure powers of love and light. The art of sparkling is a gift we must teach them early on.

My colleagues and I who work with babies have observed that new children entering the planet appear highly evolved with expanded levels of consciousness. Perhaps you have read about or know some of these Indigo children, then Crystals, Rainbow kids, Diamonds, or the newest Golden children.

As a grandmother of eight amazing grandchildren, I have also witnessed their precious hearts and the new levels of gifts they bring. They display differing levels of harmonic light and consciousness, operating much higher than their parents. They are showing us early on their genius gifts and purpose. I know that when they grow up, their higher levels of consciousness will understand the value of sparkling themselves, each other, and their world. They will develop new and advanced applications that will create a better and more loving and glorious planet.

We are all in this together with our babies leading the way. Barbara Marx Hubbard, the evolutionary educator, says we are evolving our species from homo sapiens to "homo universalis." Let us nurture and sparkle the more evolved souls of babies who may be ushering in a new golden age of light, perhaps moving us closer to embodying divinity in form.

SOLEIRA GREEN: SPARKLING NEW CONSCIOUSNESS

Extraordinary modern mystics live among us and inspire us to realize our own exceptional and infinite abilities. Soleira Green, a visionary coach, consciousness creator, author, and photographer, is a force of nature and a spectacular example of an all-knowing master who fully embodies her greatness in the most original ways. Soleira serves as a grand Sparkling Influencer to All of Life on a global and universal scale. She creates expressions of innate genius, creative innovation and quantum living. She lives in Glastonbury, England, with her husband, Santari Green, who is also a master and nutritional coach.

When working on my dissertation, I discovered this incredible woman through an internet search. Soleira has deeply influenced me to discover and share my own quantum abilities that exist in all of us. She was, coincidentally, writing about the dynamics of "alchemical dance" for coaching purposes when I was writing about the same subject, applied to the non-verbal connection and bonding of mother and baby.

We were both inspired to write about this original, important topic as one of life's organizing principles, applied in different ways. As Soleira states her book, *The Alchemical Coach*, "The dance of new leadership happens in the moment. It's an effervescent source of delight, bringing in waves of exhilaration and fulfillment to everyone it touches. Seek out all sparkling influences from the past, present and future existing in many forms that inspire and power you up to sparkle life today."

About ten years later, I got in touch with her and we have become great friends. She is probably the most magical and empowered person I have ever met, and she has inspired me to express my fullest potentials. I regularly share group conference calls for consciousness expansion with her and with other friends from around the world. We are a dedicated, powerful and impressive group of co-creators, who serve as change catalysts to promote the advancement of consciousness on the planet. These global calls are incredibly powerful!

Our collective consciousness raises each other's levels of consciousness, as we fully develop our superpower skillset. Everyone has these hidden gifts and abilities. Together we access other cosmic dimensions, receive multidimensional perspectives, holding higher vibrating frequencies, which we spread to uplift all of life. We send out our generative consciousness for greater planetary evolution and awakening.

Our committed quest is to help miraculous things occur in ever-evolving magnificence. As we have progressed in this work, we have made many shifts in our collective approach, from contacting Source energies outside of ourselves to discovering that everything, God, universes, and knowledge, can lie *within* our greater expansive Being. How exciting to witness the miraculous effects of our deepest commitment to uplift all life on this earth and in other universes for the better. Along with other lightworkers, we are collectively making profound shifts.

Soleira's visionary leadership has allowed me to bring greater amounts of crystalline light into my cells and to upgrade my DNA. This has returned my body to its original blueprint. I am enjoying greater health than in years past. I feel renewed and enthusiastic to bring sparkling to the world. You can easily shift your own consciousness to enthusiastically embrace living with a quantum perspective. You can live every moment of life each day as a conscious creator and acquire access to your infinite sparkling possibilities.

Choose to become a sparkling guardian for the light on this planet. Discover and use your innate and miraculous superpowers that you gift to the collective. This process is speeded up when you align with other like-minded souls who are doing this too. We need to form sparkling groups to take action to bring light to every corner of this world. Sparkling matters!

All these truly special teachers appeared at different points in my life to creatively fill me with the energies and rhythms of love, flow, light and authentic expression. They came quite unexpectedly, as if an unknown loving force was guiding me to fulfill my destiny. I received greater access to my own range of human potentialities, with knowledge of the human aura, expanded brain states, greater energetic abilities and higher consciousness. What amazing gifts in one lifetime that directly apply to all of us.

This knowledge now has been given to you! We hold love and light in our core that can shine like glittering jewels, whose high frequency energies we can transmit to improve the lives of all. My own sparkling was birthed into a new form. This energetic approach fans the flame to spark glowing energies to benefit life in an illuminating way.

Sparkling your Environments

"If we do not own the freshness of the air and the sparkles of the water, how can you buy them?

— Chief Seattle

YOU CAN BECOME A SPARKLER ANYTIME and express your vital energies as a form of light. Notice the ongoing give and take of energies within yourself and throughout the surroundings that you regularly frequent or are exploring. As a light steward for humanity, it is important to find ways to make even a small corner of your world sparkle for the health and happiness of our earth and all sentient beings.

Take consistent steps every day to become the best, shiniest version of yourself. It is essential for wellness to uplift the frequencies and improve the vibrational harmony within your body, home and environment. Many of us are constantly bombarded with low-level frequencies in our immediate environment, including traffic congestion, electromagnetic fields (EMFs), crowded living conditions, poor air and water quality and the effects of climate change. These accumulative effects can lead to a weakening of health with feelings of stress. What are some sparkling ideas and solutions to help revitalize?

Choose places to live and visit that invigorate you. You may be drawn to the sparkling, pristine beauty of a certain place, or you may sense the high consciousness that it holds. It is important to get out in nature, visit parks, or just spend time in your own back yard. Beauty exists endlessly in nature for our everyday upliftment.

We all have our favorite places that spark our hearts and soothe our souls. They may have sun, mountains, water, rolling hills, deserts, and lakes, or green grass and flowers. Some people like to live close to water or take beach vacations, as the negative ions in the air help the brain relax and the soothing sounds of waves lower stress levels. Notice the qualities of the energy, light and sound in your environment. Do they need a sparkling for replenishment and revitalization?

No matter where you live, create spots of beauty and send sparkles to them. Sparkling creates a blanket of good energy that can reanimate the land. There are places in nature and in my own back yard that I have sparkled over and over to create a concentration of sparkling energies.

Of course, it is important to plant more trees, clean up our water, oceans, neighborhoods, and create more community gardens for sustainable living in a compromised world. You can also use your sparkling skills for this greater good. Begin by sending out your first sparkle beam and cultivating your own inner light to generate more energetic potency. Then focus your light where you see that it needs to go. The environment needs your sparkling help!

Make positive energetic footprints with your sparkling. In *Masterful Living,* Dhyani Ywahoo, writes: "Bio-resonance is a dance.... Extraordinary people leave extraordinary waves of information in the field."

I sensed this holiness in France when visiting Chartres Cathedral and Lourdes, where for centuries people have cultivated the sacred to encourage miraculous healing. You really do feel the high vibration energies, embedded in places like the Four Corners in the Southwest of the United States, or Machu Picchu in Peru. Indigenous people for centuries have lived there and performed ceremonies to imbue the land with fertility and to create energies for collective well-being and for individual healing.

Visit sacred places to recharge with super energies in power spots, such as Mt. Shasta in California, Uluru in Australia, Mount Kalish in Tibet. These and other similar places are ultimate getaways, located on ley lines or important earth grids, imbued with strong electromagnetic currents. If you are lucky enough to visit them, you can use these energies to empower yourself.

Elevate the energies of your personal living environment. Sparklers must surround themselves with elevated vibrations in the home. As Denise Linn states in *Sacred Space*, "You are not separate from the home that you live in any more than the air you breathe. You are no less your home than your energy body. Both are outer manifestations of your inner energy fields."

Consider your home to be a sacred space. Set the mood for living with happiness and joy. Often you need to reset a home's energies, if they feel stale, by adding a splash of light. You have the power to create energetic uplift and refinement. First, clear spaces of old or stagnant energy, especially when moving into a new home.

You can do this in a variety of ways, by burning sage, sparkling rooms robustly or clearing them with a pendulum. Feel the difference this makes. Open windows and doors to circulate fresh air. Spray natural fresh-smelling mists or get a room diffuser filled with water, adding a few drops of essential oils to cleanse and purify the air.

Obviously, live green plants oxygenate the home. I always have fresh flowers or orchid plants that look lovely. I play music, sing and dance in my home to amplify positive vibrations. I communicate with my home and honor its beautiful spirit that I have actively created. Each week, I ask for the spirit of love, happiness, joy and freedom to enter my doors.

Your home is your sanctuary where you feel relaxed, comfortable and loved, away from outside pressures. Make it beautiful and inviting, so that when you enter your space, it immediately nurtures you and raises your spirits. You feel like it allows you to breathe more deeply, free from the concerns in the outer world.

I have studied *Feng Shui*, the art of spiritual placement, which has informed me about the importance of having good energy in the home. Consider such things as bed and mirror position. Moving objects of décor around on a regular basis keeps the energy circulating in rooms. Arrange decorative items differently each week, month or season for the fresh orientation. Your eyes will see novel ways to create even more beauty. Also, remember to apply these suggestions and sparkle your office and work environment.

Keeping your home sparkling clean and free of clutter helps with positive energy flow. Create more open space for higher vibrations to enter. When my spirits or emotions are down, my clothes pile up in the chair by my bed. There is an energetic feeling of disarray and neglect in the home.

I pick up around the house before I go to bed, so when I come down in the morning, I enter a fresh clean space where I can feel the spirit of love. Do not be obsessive about cleaning all the time, as that takes pleasure away from the space where you live. You must keep a balance, particularly with a family. Fewer possessions may be better.

When we moved across the country, I had to let go of many of my cherished belongings to significantly declutter our home for resale. At first, this was an agonizing process to release a life filled with so many possessions. Out of a sense of duty, I had kept antique items from family members who had passed on. They were boxed up in the basement.

The stagnant energy was palpable when the boxes were opened. I had read about the process of "tidying up" by Marie Kondo and followed her process of clearing or letting everything go that I did not absolutely love. I held each item, as she instructed, and asked myself, does it "spark joy"?

I gave a lot away and have missed none of it. My clothes were donated to help others. Immediately everything felt far more open, airy and spacious in the home, especially in my own consciousness. There was a sense of renewed freedom.

We sold our home on the first day for more than we asked. It was a gift to leave my sparkling home to another with so much cleared energy. The new owners were then ready to make a fresh start in a pristine and happy home. I reset my expectations for my new home and resolved for it to feel open and spacious, even though we would have much less living space.

It's fun to live with sparkles in your décor; they add pizzazz! My cozy sofa has an assortment of colorful pillows that I change with the seasons. One has sparkles on it. I like having crystal candlesticks with glitter candles. I am drawn to artwork and sculptures that emphasize light enhancement in their choice of shades, patches and bursts of color.

"The work of art is always based on the two poles of the onlooker and the maker, and the spark that comes from that bipolar action gives birth to something like electricity," Marcel Duchamp said.

Choose art and special objects for your home that lift your spirits and hold your personal intentions for the place. Quartz crystals and other gemstones with different spiritual-metaphysical properties add positive energies to my home and garden. There is always a big rose quartz by my desk, who is my inspirational friend. I have placed a multi-faceted hanging crystal near the front window that radiates with rainbow colors when the light hits it.

I also have created mandala-type gem grids that are purposefully constructed to send out energizing waves. They are on the carpet near skylights, where they get the sparkling effects of the sun and moonlight shining down on them. Each one carries a strong intention for my projects, and opens possibilities for the manifestation of personal goals, abundance, and renewed health and well-being. Of course, I sparkle them too!

Lighting in my home is very important because I have seasonal affective disorder (SAD). Lack of light depresses my mood and can be relieved by exposure to sunlight and bright lights. We moved to California, so I no longer suffer from winter depression. The quality of light here is truly beautiful as imbued with a kind of translucency. I always have full spectrum light bulbs in my lamps. Hanging little sparkle lights both inside and on the patio makes everyone feel the light of any season.

Setting up a small home altar is a sacred act that keeps you close to Divine consciousness. The intention is for it to help continuously bless and raise the frequency of your home and office. You can receive guidance from Source and Higher Beings of Light. You just need to ask.

On your altar you can place pictures of religious figures or goddesses, or friends who are special and require some prayers, and other meaningful objects. You can burn devotional candles or incense and place flowers nearby. My friend plays continuous musical mantras sung by different artists on her CD player to elevate the frequencies near her altar.

Sparkling goes together with keeping a spirit of gratitude and thankfulness. My home has a wall filled with happy family pictures, which make me feel grateful, joyous and energized. All these creative ideas enhance your sparkling life with the goodness of your inspirations and loved ones.

On a more fun topic, what do you wear that uplifts you? Your clothing and style can make you feel happy. The fashion industry uses many sparkle sequins and shiny fabrics to create a fun and glamorous effect. I love to wear my sparkle flip flops and I own two different sequined sets of Micky Mouse ears, given to me by my adorable granddaughter, who knows me well. I love my hot pink sweater, orange vest, turquoise sneakers, casual shirts with shiny threads, and colorful workout tights.

Long ago, Jack Schwartz taught me to change from work clothes into something more flowing when I return from work. This helps me shift from my beta logical mind to a more creative alpha mind for relaxation in the evening. He suggested wearing shoes with leather on the soles, not rubber, to better absorb the frequencies from the earth. This was an awesome suggestion. My favorite shoes are my boots and hand-made sandals from France with leather soles, because of the added energy that they provide me during the day.

We know about the health benefits of "earthing." Take your shoes off and go barefoot in the grass to pick up the natural and uplifting frequencies. Also, you can wear sparkling earrings, necklaces and fun shades of nail polish to boost your glow and sparkle factor!

Wearing jewels and living with gems can expose you to their many attributes and wisdom from connection to the mineral kingdom. Every day I wear a lavender jade ring and a pink-red fire opal necklace that emits tiny bright sparks that I feel uplift my energy on many levels. These small colorful jewelry items are beautiful and make me feel happy and protected by their high emitting frequencies.

These suggestions are mostly personal. You will find your own ways to consider adding a dash of sparkle to your home that lights you up every moment. With intention you can spread good vibrations to your neighborhood, city, state, county and planet. Send out sparkling energies help to clear collective fear and negative energies. Your love and light can offer help to make a big difference!

> *"If there be righteousness in the heart,*
> *there will be beauty in character,*
> *If there be beauty in character,*
> *there will be harmony in the home,*
> *If there be harmony in the home,*
> *there will be order in the nation,*
> *If there be order in the nation,*
> *there will be peace in the world."*
>
> — Confucius

Sparkling for Health and Vitality

"We are radiant beings. We need to shine forth this radiance which actually brings forth a state of health and wholeness. Health is an evolutionary state."

— Jack Schwartz

SPARKLING IS A NEW ENERGY PRACTICE that can help transform your health and vitality! You hold sparkling mastery in your hands. Sparkling raises your vibrations the more that you do it. Let's boost personal health and immune functioning by intentionally strengthening the light in our physical bodies, biofields and/or light bodies. I make no claims for sparkling as a healing modality. It can complement medical care. It doesn't replace it.

We must all elevate our frequencies, because our modern technological world is constantly depleting our energies with vibrational density and environmental pollutants. Collective energies of fear and low vibration can cause energetic imbalances/disharmonies in our energy fields. According to Jarrad Hewett in *Energy is the Answer*, "Our own physical nature and energy fields are in a desperate need of a reboot."

Consciously sparkle yourself frequently to brighten up the internal landscapes of your mind, body, and heart. Sometimes I feel tingles or goosebumps from this energetic uplift. Visualize your cells, organs and center column receiving the brightest light! Can you feel the difference?

Here are some other practical ways to improve your health:

GET SOME SUN: Give yourself light infusions. Sunlight causes your body to produce Vitamin D.

PLUG INTO SOURCE: Call on inexhaustible energies from Source, both within and without. Let these energies flow into your head and down your spine, then ground light into the earth through your feet.

BREATHE: Pause and take long, deep breaths. Calm yourself.

MOVE YOUR BODY: Relax, move, stretch, wiggle and shake. Circulate your energy.

LIGHTEN UP: Be in the flow. Listen to happy tunes and to high vibrational music.

CLEAR YOUR ENERGY FIELDS: Eat healthy foods, cultivate happiness and joy, meditate, and sparkle, intend to clear yourself, chakras and energy fields. Use visualizations.

EXPAND YOUR CONSCIOUSNESS: Access your Infinite Self. Get excited about real life and soul pursuits. Love and laugh.

These simple steps can improve your general well-being just by using your intent, imagination and applying action steps. Sparkling daily is a great addition to your health regimen! Sparkle yourself head to toe with bright light to stay in high vibration. Physically send yourself light using your hands or just visualize this. This is a preventative measure. This allows you to clear any low vibrations, when you are feeling depleted, stressed or unwell, and then boosts your light exponentially with high energy sparkles and intentions. Sparkling creates beneficial energetic shifts. Each small shift builds upon the one before to upgrade your health, happiness and well-being. Elevating the quality of your own light also serves your health and well-being.

When I think I am coming down with a cold, besides taking vitamin C, I always give myself a series of strong sparklings and visualize running colored lights (golden, pink, blue green, violet and white lights) My body knows what colors it needs and which locations need specific shades of light. This act prepares me both physically and emotionally to proactively fight off the virus. Sending this intense light helps my immune system work better on my best behalf. My attitude becomes positive to alleviate my worry about my condition. Send different colored sparkles to your atoms, cells, organs, chakras and biofields. Send sparkles into your entire neural network of your brain. Infuse your arteries, blood and life force with sparkling energies.

I use sparkles in different ways to both enhance my energies and to recalibrate my health to a higher frequency. I infuse glistening sparkles into my vitamins, foods and drinking water. I imagine receiving glistening sparkles in the waters out of the shower head during my showers. Think of ways to include sparkles in your health and beauty regimens.

Your body-mind is a field of awareness and sensing this unity furthers your sparkling health, no matter your health situation. You are the best person to sense your own energetic levels, feelings, thoughts, tensions, and bodily needs. These states are always in flux, so you need to pay attention. Tune in to see if sparkles of love and light are needed and where to apply them. This awareness is key to restoring your sparkling health. The essence of health is positively engaging your body-mind-spirit to pave the way to a happier, healthy life.

You have a choice of where to put your attention and energy. Joy increases enthusiasm and strengthens your life force. Notice what lifts you up and what doesn't. Your health greatly benefits when you can change the way you habitually react to events that trigger you. Separate your response from the circumstance. Fatigue and reactivity can drain your life force and negatively impact your health. These conditions affect your sparkling potency. To change your feelings, become aware of them, acknowledge them fully, and then release them into the light.

Notice when you are experiencing internal emotional disharmony or stress, and then clear any associated energetic congestion. Sparkle yourself robustly to blast this out. Then follow up by gently applying sparkles for restoration or rejuvenation. I sparkle myself, when I feel like complaining and need an inspirational reminder to stay positive. Open spaces for your light to shine from your entire being.

Sparkling helps you awaken positive feelings that fuel happiness and pleasure over negativity. Also, I invite joyful and harmonic frequencies into my own consciousness. Dial into the vibratory state of your natural bliss of being. Elevate yourself to rise in higher frequencies to shine and sparkle your world. Transmit sparkling energies to circulate bright light through your biofields, body, mind, heart, spirit and soul. You can become lighter, more open and alive. These emotional transformations support your physical body and your auric fields for greater clarity and happiness.

We are energetic beings who want to feel light, vital and sparkly. Good health with its glow is your original birthright. It's beautiful to witness people who have sparkling eyes, hair, skin, teeth, enhanced by a positive personality. Sparkling energies make you appear effervescent, youthful and more present. People see you as healthy and attractive, no matter your age, and as someone others want to be around. Think of ways to include sparkles in your health and beauty regimens.

Beauty is more than skin deep. Real beauty is about discovering your inner light and expressing its luminosity from your heart. You become a vessel of living, glowing, positive energy that emanates self-esteem and genuine goodness. People notice when you have a bright energetic presence that reflects an expansive light field. This alchemy of love and light enhances your bare-naked radiance, which shines from compassionate heart and from your healthy cells.

Sparkling has become my philosophy of life and it can become yours too! Beam out your light and notice and feel the light of others. In *Discovering your Soul Signature,* Panashe Desai, states: "Along with being aware of this light within you, notice that everyone you encounter during the day is accompanied by this light. See the goodness in everyone you meet. Catch their radiance as if it is a sunbeam."

Throughout your sparkling journey, you gradually move from a focus on personal attractiveness to truly fully loving yourself, which motivates you to care for your total being on physical, etheric and energetic levels. You generally take better care of yourself when you feel energized to eat nurturing foods, get more rest, exercise, walk, and do yoga or dance. When you are nurturing yourself, you feel able to concentrate on boosting life energies through sparkling.

Sparkling is an easy, energetic way to rejuvenate another's energies for their improved physical, emotional and spiritual health. Remember to ask them if they would like your sparkling ministration first. The good news is that it fortifies both the vitality of the sparkler and transforms those being sparkled. The wonderful thing about sparkling is that it is dynamically reciprocal. Sending out good will, love and light can purify and energize you, while boosting another's life force. This is a win-win. You become equipped with new skills and gain self-sufficiency, without constant reliance non other energetic practitioners.

I receive many requests from others to sparkle energies to encourage better health. One day, a woman asked me to sparkle her in her shop. She had experienced a bad fall the day before and had gone to the hospital for X-rays. Nothing was broken, but her hip and back were in great pain. I walked around her, flicking my hands to send golden sparkles to her hip, back, and heart. Afterward, she looked visibly brightened and we both laughed with this sense of relief. The next day, she called to say her pain was almost entirely gone. I saw that my sparkles released her anxiety and that she had benefitted from my quick, empathic response. The sparkles seemed to do the trick!

As you continue to practice sparkling, you lighten up your ego involvement. You grow and change and evolve. There is a point when you realize you are not your beliefs, thoughts, emotions or actions, but a soul who is loving and already wise. You lose your old hardened identity of trying to control others for your own needs and benefits, which is exhausting.

Relax into a vast knowing of consciousness, where your vast stores of light and effervescent essence await you! Take the time to commune with expansive inner light that is ascending into greater spirals of luminosity. You consciously enter realms of higher vibrations, where you can enter states of ecstasy. Enlightenment comes when you are involved in a fusing of bodily and spiritual knowing that shifts your perceptions, orientation and consciousness to a higher order of vital being and functioning. In *Cosmic Consciousness* Mark Prophet writes, "I come to make you sun-centers—to increase the decibels of consciousness to a new dimension of cosmic awareness."

Drop into your heart and connect to your higher self from multidimensional perspectives. From this greater vantage point, you live with elevated frequencies that invigorate your body, mind, spirit and soul. The more you awaken your greater depths of inner love and light, the more energetic enhancement you experience. You feel so much gratitude for the greater support received from Light servers in the higher planes of existence. Your daily sparkling practice helps you discover pristine, blissful energetic states that expand your light reserves. At higher dimensions, bask in the glorious glow and dance of the light fantastic!

"Future Medicine will be the Medicine of frequencies."
— Albert Einstein

Sparkling for Dark Times

*"I will love the light for it shows me the way; I
will love the darkness for it shows me the stars."*

—Og Mandino

THE COSMOS CONTAINS BOTH LIGHT AND DARKNESS. The sun
streams great amounts of light onto our planet that sustains us.
Dark energy and dark matter in the unmanifested realms of
the void make up most of the mass of the universe. Vast areas
of darkness are filled with stars, galaxies and other universes
composed mostly of this dark matter, dark energy and black
holes. The void is a primordial place holding great generative
power. For example, human babies develop in the darkness
of the womb to be born into a world of light. Creation and
mystery arise from the black void. There was the darkness
before God created light: "Darkness was on the face of the
deep. And the Spirit of God moved." (Genesis 1:2)

A sparkler must honor these perspectives by staying
mindful that, like the universe, our lives contain periods of
light and dark. During some periods in life, new ideas may
be germinating inside of you, not fully formed. It is good to

understand when you are in an incubation phase, stage in the creative process. Your personal creations are not yet ready to spring forth to bloom in the light of day. There is appreciation for the unseen manifesting power of the void. Any sparkler can replenish himself, when entering the stillness of the void.

The sparkler can move energies from Source, containing the generative powers of the void, to elevate frequencies for continuing positive change. The main job of a dedicated sparkler is to bring light and hope to dark times and places, with no judgment. This act creates ripples that can cause sparkles to shower on people, animals and places. You can easily learn to sparkle to serve life. This restorative art of sparkling is applied with love, light and wisdom, but requires discernment. It is important to differentiate the potentials received from the creative void from those external, negative forces that are disruptive and harmful. The latter do not resonate with the frequencies of love.

Throughout human history into the modern world, many dark situations, conflicts and events have caused serious harmful misalignment to human health and psyche. What are some of these negative forces? They range from intentional prejudice, hatred, injustice, ignorance and greed to environmental disasters, pandemics, war and mass killings, which cause destruction and collective fear. Other non-beneficial factors, large and small, can hinder healthy living and cause imbalances in human vital energies. For example, one can suffer physically and emotionally from negative personal interactions and abuse, illness and disease, poor and insufficient nutrition. Even the effects of EMFs from phones, TVs and microwaves, can disrupt our emotions and the health of biofields. The good news is that sparkling helps to clear these discordant energies to introduce beautiful shades of love, light and compassion to the world. This practice can be essential to restore vibrational harmony, balance and wellness.

In my early thirties, I experienced a series of unexpected emotional setbacks that completely overwhelmed me. In quick succession, everything darkened and my light, happy world turned dark. I became sick with several illnesses, had a near-death surgery, experienced the loss of a baby, the early death of my mother, and a divorce. These events catapulted me into great personal pain and suffering. I became seriously depressed and dramatically lost weight. Sometimes, it seemed as if I entered an unfamiliar landscape and didn't know my way home. I felt isolated and scared. It was such an awful period that I consciously chose to dim my light, which lowered my vibrations and made things worse.

Never hide your light, or put it in a box, or think that you are all alone. You are always connected to Source and to love. There is really nothing to fear.

I have learned that life's dark currents must be acknowledged, felt, and navigated with grace. These dark times can yield amazing treasures. It takes courage to move through inner and outer darkness. You need to use your intuition in difficult periods and to continue to sparkle light, so you can see and confront your own issues. When facing my own dark night of the soul, I soon realized that life has both light and dark moments.

Bad things can happen to good people. I had no influence over some personally devastating events. I did have control over how I responded to major disappointments and setbacks. It is best to surrender to the things that cannot be changed and find ways to change the things that you can. With therapeutic help, many of my repressed emotions that came from earlier experiences, related to fears, disappointment, pain, grief and rage, were released. I became aware of my own self-criticism and need for perfection and relationships that drained my energies and needed to end.

Let's not add to collective darkness. Embrace your own dark side to release those traits, limitations, and layers of emotional and cellular density that may hurt yourself and others. As Carl Jung said: "There is no coming to consciousness without pain. One does not become enlightened by imagining figures of light, but rather by making conscious what is darkness."

There are many times when you are blindsided by unexpected little things that trigger old wounds and early feelings of inadequacy. Eventually, my depression lifted as I gained more self-awareness and took responsibility to not consider myself a victim. I was dedicated to help myself and become healthy and strong so I could raise my young daughters. Slowly, this recovery and painful transition changed the course of my life. My greatest discoveries during these difficult times were:

Do not force anything to happen.

Relax and take good care of yourself.

Slow down, breathe and reflect.

Raise your vibration whenever possible.

Discern clearly what you are dealing with in the muck.

Embrace the darkness within. Move inward to become aware of old emotions and patterns that need to be cleared. Discover light within your own heart.

Ask for help and use your growing resources.

Cultivate your dedication to the Spirit of Light.

There were more lessons and personal insights to be learned. I had a home robbery shortly after this dark period. Beautiful jewelry I had inherited and truly treasured, including a valuable diamond ring, necklace and bracelet, were gone forever. However, this loss caused me to reflect even more about myself and to take action to empower myself. I saw that some of my self-worth was related to having these special material possessions.

This awareness caused me to make a huge psychological shift. I realized that there were sparkling diamonds inside of me that could be unearthed and used for greater service. I had inner talents that still had not been cultivated and I needed to take greater charge of my career options and spiritual avenues.

My aspiration to unearth more precious jewels inside myself changed the course of my life. These inner sparkling gems would be much more valuable than having any real jewels kept in a safe. I knew in my deepest soul that expanding my own "bare-naked radiance" was my next level of growth. This caused me to pivot my dance therapy career and move in a new direction. I moved out of my comfort zone. My new resolve brought more energy to my life.

My life goal to dig deeper led me to return to school to pursue my doctorate, which eventually led to my development of energetic sparkling for the betterment of humanity. From a dark period, a new direction emerged. I found more ways to use my talents for the benefit of others. My education gave me many tools to help others face their own darkness. My heart expanded to become a guide who helped others navigate the shadows of their psyche and release early trauma stored in the body. I was familiar with the territory.

When the time is right, you may want to consciously explore your old programming that added to patterns of personal wounding. Hold onto curiosity to spot these patterns as you go deeper to discover their personal and intergenerational origins. Letting go of old stories to become a new, lighter version of your original blueprint is a worthy process. I love the verse in Leonard Cohen's song, "There is a crack in everything and that is how the light comes in." Keep your divine spark ignited, like the pilot light on your stove. This fuller flame serves to both purify you and as well as light up all parts of you. It helps to burn away any heaviness from old programming, negatively charged life issues, habits and influences that need to be cleared and released. It fully motivates you to embody all your light. A personal healing journey leads you to revitalization with the freedom to shine as your true authentic self.

Here are some resources to stay resilient:

Cultivate your own self-love in response
 to pain/disappointments.

Practice self-care to vitalize your well-being.

Summon your courage.

Be open to make changes in your life.

Do what you fear the most. (As an academic
 person, I was reluctant to come out in the
 world as a sparkler for fear of ridicule).

Lighten up and keep your sense of humor.

Pay attention and choose positive thoughts,
 words, habits and actions.

Express daily gratitude for your life.

Sparkling is a terrific resource in times of darkness. It helps to brighten you, no matter what the circumstance, to elevate your frequencies. You can make a huge difference as a sparkler as you apply your light, but please do so consciously. Become aware of your boundaries and possible overstepping as to try to help others.

Guard your light when you must. Lavish it when you receive permission to spread it. Sparklers can learn to discern when damaging darkness is present. Also, when you sense or clearly see what is going on inside yourself, you no longer serve as a naive "do-gooder," someone who projects their own darkness onto others in the name of the light. It is important to release any potential negativity that clouds your interpersonal fields or your work. There is always more to clear, so that more of your great light can shine more brightly.

Do not allow yourself to stay discouraged. Exposure to both light and dark moments furthers your awareness and personal growth. You gather strength and resources and learn how to access the unlimited potentials that make rainbows! Live and create expansive light in this world. Hopefully this will become a revolution.

> *"You have to dance through the dark in order to see the light. You have to go to the source of all of our wounds, the big wound, the divorce of the spirit from flesh, and heal this wound if you ever want to fulfill the longing for a real self, a soulful self, a big, huge self, one that sleeps with the Beloved."*
> — Gabrielle Roth

SPARKLING AS A SPIRITUAL PRACTICE

*"As you experience your own body, mind, and spirit,
becoming more and more full of light, experience
that the darkness in front of you is beginning to
drain away. As you blaze more and more, so the
light becomes more and more intense in the darkness
before you, until, when you are completely alight,
you and the light, from one horizon to the other,
are one light, one diamond light blazing."*

— Andrew Harvey, *Return of the Mother*

SPARKLING CAN BECOME your new spiritual practice to center and restore you. Taking time to pause from life's busy distractions helps you build personal coherence and receive insights. Many people practice mindfulness, yoga or prayer as spiritual practices to empty the mind, encourage a peaceful heart and support body-mind wholeness. We need a wider variety of options that inspire us to pursue our own evolving spiritual growth. The practice of sparkling allows you to acquire another resource and skill to evolve your greater spiritual mastery.

Some of us don't feel comfortable with a sitting meditation alone. I generally prefer moving meditations. For over forty-five years, authentic movement has been my preferred practice. It became my mainstay to relax and allow for natural movement expression of my unfolding inner life. As I explored sparkling more deeply, I realized that it has its own wealth of contemplative benefits. With regular sparkling practice, you become a refined instrument of Source, deeply immersed in light. You sometimes receive upgrades of light transmissions that inform your practice, and inspire your thoughts and ideas, and expand your consciousness.

Both the practices of sparkling, authentic movement and yoga foster greater awareness and ground you in the present moment. Both use movement to access flow states that energize your health and fuel your spiritual renewal. For me, the interplay of these practices produces new spiraling insightful revelations.

The spiritual practice of sparkling has both active and passive elements. It can stir your spirit, move your body, hands and fingers to transmit light, while quieting the mind as you enter a flow state. Here are some of the benefits of pursuing sparkling as your daily practice:

Connection to the quantum Source of creation and to all life.

Conscious awareness of intuition and bodily wisdom.

Creative involvement.

Cultivation of inner light and energetic vitality.

Unique expression of your authentic self.

Engagement of body, mind, spirit and soul.

Stress release through play, flowing movement,
and spontaneity.

Creation of limitless possibilities for serving
others and life.

There are different ways to use sparkling as a spiritual practice. You can do a sitting meditation, which centers you by simply focusing on the light that you are.

It's like looking at a campfire and feeling drawn in by the flames and their captivating beauty. You can meditate on your radiant divine spark within, which is accessed deep within your heart. Focus on expanding this light inside of you to illuminate all your cells and your entire being. Extend this inner light further out to encompass your auric field and keep expanding this light to go where it is needed in the world. When you become aware of the magnitude of the light that you are, you can sparkle brighter in the world. As you cultivate your light, you build up a radiant concentration over time that allows your entire presence to shine like the rays of the glorious sun.

My favorite daily sparkling practice is a walking meditation, throughout all seasons. You can use this special time to witness your world without judgment and look with eyes of appreciation and wonder. It allows you to deepen your relationship with life! Sparkle with your moving hands, to honor and bless what you perceive. Your consciousness follows this expressive dance in light. As a dedicated sparkler, you grow in competency to increase light and to uplift its frequencies. Sparkling walks help to clear and quiet your mind, so you can give your full presence to others. The practice itself is very grounding and settles your nervous system. You tap into a complete stillness within. This stillness at times takes you into a void or zero point, where you experience an incomprehensible power that can express a greater multidimensional, energetic light through you.

A sparkling walk feels so refreshing too! It feels good physically and can keep your torso flexible and your arms, hands and fingers supple. You can be "the universe in ecstatic motion," as Rumi so beautifully stated. Just walk out your door and become the dance of all possibilities. Sparkling goes wherever you go, and you don't have to be anywhere special to practice. Sparkle everything that moves you—trees, plants, grasses, bunnies, birds, bugs or people—whatever is present to you during this time. Combine rhythmic walking with opening your consciousness to put you in a creative alpha or theta state. You enjoy a new sense of peace and playfulness. Your heart's desire stays connected to a higher level of service as you extend light to others to inspire physical and spiritual well-being. *Be all that you are and can be.*

Sparkling as a spiritual practice makes you keenly aware of the ever-changing play of light that exists everywhere you look. It feels like a practice-within-a-practice just to observe the ineffable light that nature presents that you noticed with so many subtleties and variations. This activity heightens all your senses. For example, I feel entranced by the dappled light on trees, luminous clouds, colors of the sky, the intensity of the sunlight, the shining vibrance of light on the water, and their contrasts with each other. Sparkling in this way has helped my birdwatching skills, as I notice more details. Constant viewing and meditating on the light inspire you to transmit new combinations of light using your sparkling intention and artistry. Become aware of the light that connects all things within and without. Express its higher resonance that both sparks and moves you. Serve yourself and others with your sparkling light.

Like most spiritual practices, sparkling fosters personal transformation and experiences of serenity. The benefits are many. As you enter more deeply into the process, sparkle shifts occur that spontaneously increase levels of flow, moments of clarity, and heart expansion. Witness your personal changes as you breathe deeply. You will feel comfortable when you realize you can make moment-to-moment bodily and energetic shifts.

"Breathe in your heart and believe in yourself" is my personal motto. Sparkling allows you to shift your brain hemispheres by consciously moving from left brain logical states to right brain creative states. You shift from mind-only logic to heart-centered knowing and continue to shift your perceptions from details to bigger picture, quantum living. This moves you out of a duality mindset to embrace Oneness, with interconnections to all living things. The great news is, with every sparkle shift made you are choosing sovereignty over being a victim in your life, to increase your pleasure, enhance self-care, and support your fullest possibilities.

Your spiritual sparkling practice builds up your body with light. You add to the radiance of others as you serve them from your inner place of love. It honors the Divine Feminine aspect of God, whose basic love principle nurtures life. With each sparkle, you send out a creational wave to initiate something new in the dance of life. In *Voices of Our Ancestors,* Dhyani Ywahoo, writes: "And we are each pregnant with a new world. Each of us is carrying the seed of a planetary unity and a great peace that has not been seen for thousands and thousands of years."

Each sparkling moment returns you to the innocence of a child who looks through eyes of delight. The sparkler is simultaneously a compassionate parent who expresses unconditional love by deeply caring for all offspring.

Consider trying this new, uplifting spiritual practice. Cultivate your bright and clear energetic presence that positively affects others. You become, as Stephen Vincent Benet said, "bright streams of water watering to the world."

As you raise your own vibrations and those whom you are sparkling, your conscious sparkling moves both you and life to operate to a more harmonic key. The beauty of regular sparkling is that it keeps you growing and evolving in its endless art.

> *"The awareness of the Body of Light and the capacity to enhance and to use it has to be guided by something else. Something else is the capacity to suspend our horizontal lifestyle and to reach out vertically into something that is beyond our daily activities, even for a moment."*
>
> — Dona Holleman, *Dancing the Body of Light*

Supernova Sparkling

*"In a supernova of consciousness, Gaia and her children
will ascend in robes of light, forming a luminous
lightbody of love, to be reborn among the stars."*

— Ariel Spilsbury and Michael Bryner

THE HIGHEST ART OF SPARKLING is a form of light mastery I call
supernova sparkling. The definition of a supernova is "a star
that suddenly increases in brightness because of an explosion
that ejects most of its mass." As Richard Rudd describes in
Gene Keys, "The elements of your body were made in the
stars, and you turn back into a star in your mini supernova."
Express the purest fire and brightest light of your body and
soul through advanced sparkling.

Your open heart and jubilant spirit create a palpable
vibrancy that magnifies the invisible brilliance sent forth
from your hands. Your clear intent and heightened energies
can send waves of sparkling diamond light everywhere, even
to unimaginable places. Get excited by these new inspiring
possibilities. Ask yourself if this supernova sparkling serves

your own highest divine choice and soul? You will clearly know. Your joyful engagement enhances the potency and range of your supernova sparkling skills for the benefit of yourself and everyone.

This chapter is meant to teach people who are ready to learn about ways to take sparkling to the next level. Not everyone wants to do this. Enjoy sparkling at whatever level you are comfortable with.

Supernova sparkling is the mastery level in which you exhibit finer levels of awareness and abilities. It fully uses your gift of gratitude that cultivates divine presence. You become the transformation. Here are the steps that raise your sparkling to higher planes:

Open your heart more fully and awaken to
    greater depths of love.

Dedicate yourself to your own highest good
    as you serve others.

Deepen your connection to your intuition
    linked to Source.

Enhance, build and strengthen your overall
    "bare-naked radiance."

Apply colors to your sparkling for greater impact.

Transmit forcefields of light and sacred Flames.

In this book, I have taught you basic sparkling skills to transmit light for the benefit yourself and those around you. After you master the basic practice, you become ready to use your increased sparkling powers in more potent and creative ways. By practicing sparkling and/or engaging in other forms of meditation or personal growth activities, you have acquired personal clarity and experiential knowledge of light activities.

You are ready to learn and perfect more skills.

You begin to fully love yourself through your advanced engagement, that exponentially overflows to life and to your sparkling! With mastery, you can take your sparkling to new heights and spheres of benevolent influence! As your skills evolve with dedicated practice, you become a *mover of life and spirit,* then a *master of light.*

At advanced stages, you begin to function like a musical conductor, who harmonizes different energies into unity to create a new song. As Jarrad Hewitt states in *The Answer is Energy*: "Energy powers every incandescent bulb, candle, sparkler, lightning bug and twinkle light. It is your source of power to illuminate the world and broadcast your beautiful symphony for all to hear." You can evolve your sparkling to a high art that resonates with a new octave. Expect a deeper connection to Source, to self-love with increased dedication to serve life.

Full-spectrum sparkling abilities begin through a merger of your great love with your great light, aligned with a greater Source. Loving yourself and others fuels your Light expansion. As your love and light energies are amplified, you may experience more synchronicities. Surprising manifestations can occur out of the blue. Your personal power shifts as you operate as a field of consciousness, rather than through ego alone. Your sparkling encourages you to connect more deeply with a higher power or Source that connects all things and is an inner path to enlightenment. Communion with your Higher Self supports expression of your soul design to serve your divine purpose.

You are inspired to consistently operate at a higher level of integrity and love. You serve with expanded consciousness, less motivated by personal gain. You become engaged in both generative action and compassionate witnessing. You feel closer to people all over the world, as you share and sparkle with unity consciousness.

During this time of personal advanced sparkling exploration, you will experience ongoing shifts of personal consciousness power and embodiment with new intuitive perceptions. It feels good to stay more in touch with your inner core. You utilize your intuition more strongly to know what is needed, when sparkling another person or situation. Please pay attention and become aware of you inner, bodily messages and feelings coming from your heart, brain, and gut intelligences. With attunement, each area of intelligence can offer a message or feeling sense. For example, you may get a gut knowing, or heart calling to pause or act. Notice when you feel a harmonic alignment of all three intelligences that creates a clear coherent channel of knowing. You then become greatly empowered in your actions, because the love, wisdom and truth received from within, are connected to higher divine guidance.

Honestly, I often turn off my thoughts and let currents of love and light lead me to either, be, relax or do. This is a reminder that the depths of your heart intelligence are greater than your brain. With no mental resistance, you more easily enter flow states and feel light-heartedness. This makes your sparkling more fun and fluid, because you feel in harmony with natural forces.

As your enhanced sparkle power grows, your body hums with vital power. You are utilizing more energies that expand your biofields, along with their luminosity. Your dedication to your light expansion can take you into greater dimensions of light. Your consciousness enters fields and holy places filled with sparkling light and realms of diamonds.

The great news is that your own bare-naked radiance expands its range of illumination with a strengthening of your light. When I made the commitment to uncover the diamonds inside of me twenty years ago, I never imagined that my dearest wish would come true! My unique essence shines brightly as lustrous diamonds that reveals many clear and brilliant facets that reflect heaven on earth.

As a supernova sparkler, you become an artist, attuned to beauty in the moment who can consciously choose to sparkle with different colors. You creatively discern what colors to send with each sparkling encounter. There are many ways to match your sparkling colors to the needs of the receiver. What sparkling effects are you trying to achieve? Is your aim to energize or cheer up, create a glow or brighten, create growth or potency, soothe or release and or cleanse or purify? Choose and discern which colors may be the most appropriate to transmit.

You can research color therapy to discover which colors are healing for different groups and environments. In my opinion, the colors of reds and golds send vigor, light pinks and honey gold send sweetness, purple lights send royal richness, greens are refreshing and provide balance, blues and whites are calming, yellows and corals brighten, and oranges invigorate and remove fatigue.

For example, I love to sparkle roses with a soft wave of pure white light to express my appreciation for their beauty. I usually flick robust golden light energies to trees in short successive bursts to express joy for their strength and wisdom. You begin to get an intuitive feeling for the precise color to send to each plant or person. If you send a blue color for inner peace, should it be a royal blue, pale blue, aqua, turquoise, or periwinkle? Tune into the colors to see them with your inner eye, then you'll know which one is right. You also learn how much light energy to send. There are no mistakes. Keep exploring endlessly just for fun!

Create your own magical light mixes! Do you realize you can sparkle sunlight and starlight, because we are intimately connected to everything in the whole universe? As Charan Surdhar said, "When you move your fingers, you tickle the stars."

Use your imagination to infuse Divine sparks with pure love, stardust, moonbeams, rainbows, crystalline glow, fiery power, diamond light, rainbow light, moonlight, lovelight and colored flames. Each mixture, or elixir, carries a different frequency and creates a different desired effect of sparkling loveliness. Feel the alchemy of these new creations in your body and soul. Send out intentional bursts of lights using a swirling kaleidoscope of coloration.

Stand up for what is important to you! Mastering your abilities to work with light makes you feel more empowered and willing to discover many successful applications for your skills. Create infusions that offer different qualities and alchemical potencies to meet the needs of your recipient or situation. How big can you dream? Your powerful heart and light can emit love filled chemistries that may impact the flowering and nurture of the seeds of life. How big can you dream? Who knows if supernova sparkling can cause changes for biodiversity? Your growing skillset gives you the power to make a difference. For example, you can intentionally set up a forcefield or pillar of light to surround a person, home, animal or community for the purposes of love or for their protection from viruses and flu, illness or devasting weather events. I have found this to be quite an effective intervention. Take action in times of need.

At the highest level, you can transmit potent Flames from your hands and fingers. This a high-powered and sacred extension of sparkling. Tellis S. Papastavro, in *The Gnosis and the* Law, says, "The Flame is a power, a substance and intelligent force." The Flames represent the sacred vibrations of God. This spiritual activity is practiced by some dedicated lightworkers. I consider it another level of spiritual dedication, knowledge and mastery.

Determine clearly what you are desiring and needing the Flames to do and manifest. They are transmitted in times of environmental and human catastrophes and pandemics, sent to any location on the planet as a powerful resource. The various Flames come from the Seven Rays of Light, have varying jewel toned colors, frequencies and qualities, sending a different effect and action. Their job may be one of clearing, transmuting darkness, purifying etc.

It is good to understand different Flame applications and to know the Light Beings in charge of them. Invoke each specific Flame with powerful conviction, calling on the powerful Presence of God or its ministering Archangel or Ascended Master. As your hands powerfully transmit these sacred invisible Flames, use your strong heart-felt feelings to magnetize or charge up your intended actions. Be assured that these powerful flames blaze but never burn. Know with certainty that they will accomplish what you have commanded them to do through the grace of God.

Many lightworkers know the benefits of using the powerful Violet Flame. It has a violet coloration of a brilliant amethyst gem. Its sacred fire is powerfully invoked for transmutation, mercy and forgiveness. Saint Germain is known as an Ascended Master who is a Guardian for this remarkable Violet Flame. I have used it to offset and minimize the effects of environmental storms, disasters and flooding in different areas of the globe. This work is powerful when done as a collective offering this.

The Blue Flame is a beautiful sapphire light and is associated with Archangel Michael, used for powerful ministration to reduce chaos and negativity. The Green Flame is a deep emerald color, associated with Archangel Raphael, used for divine healing. The Yellow Flame carries a bright, golden illumination, associated with Archangel Jophiel, used for divine wisdom, abundance and illumination. The White Flame is a diamond crystalline white, associated with Archangel Gabriel and is associated with purity. I love to send out the White Flames, which feel electric, to cleanse world sickness from viral epidemics and disease to restore purity and balance. The Pink Flame is crystalline rose colored light, associated with Archangel Chamuel and is sent to bring beauty, divine love, compassion and adoration. I use this flame often to dispel fear and panic and restore love and grace in the atmosphere. Lastly, the Ruby Flame is associated with Archangel Uriel, offering service to Humanity for enlightened spiritual understanding and peace

By mastering supernova sparkling, you can become a force for change in infinite ways. Let's sparkle through the best and worst of times. Stay strong in your inner light so you can share it with others. Extend your powerful light in supernova sparkling capacities, sent out as pure expressions to serve each other and to illuminate, cleanse and beautify our world.

> *"In the name of the Fire,*
> *The Flame,*
> *And the Light!*
> *Praise the pure presence of fire*

That burns from within
Without thought of time.
... May courage
Cause our lives to flame
In the name of the Fire,
And the Flame,
And the Light."

— John O'Donohue

Perspectives on Sparkling

*"The key to all you would accomplish in this
lifetime hinges upon your willingness to embrace all
that you are, for the chance that you may come to
experience—in Oneness—all that you truly Are."*

— Rasha

HAVE YOU EVER NOTICED that sparkles in nature look like
glimmering waves of diamond lights dancing across the ocean
or a sea of shining stars in the nighttime sky? When I see
sparkles like these, I feel mesmerized, drawn in, and inspired
by their glowing, scintillating light. They uplift your feelings.
Your soul is moved. They remind us that we do not exist in
isolation, but live together as different families of beautiful
lights, infinitely connected in the web of life. Let's preserve
the natural glow of life and keep our ecosystems strong
and shining bright with health, not diminished by draining
circumstances. Sparkling is both inspirational and a practical
tool to enhance life's radiance. Energies are offered to
strengthen the light connection that energizes and brightens
all interconnected systems.

CHOOSE TO ENERGIZE YOURSELF AND LIFE. Sparkling is clearly an energetic enhancer that raises vibration, pure and simple. When you are sparkling, you don't visually see the energies coming out of your heart, hands and body, but you feel the joy from these light transmissions in your cells. This small gesture offers more than you think! Others remark that they feel the energetic support when the positive vibrations are sent to them. My practice of sparkling has inspired me to live a happy, healthy lifestyle. I feel younger and revitalized. This means of self-empowerment has improved my life, creating joy-filled moments. As I have developed sparkling as my practice, I have gradually noticed the amazing benefits of working with light to hold a high vibration both for myself and others. I have used it as a tool for personal growth and change, as I play with infinite possibilities. Expanding my efforts to create positive energetic horizons for the world is also important, meaningful and fun!

USE SPARKLING TO LET SOMEONE KNOW THAT YOU CARE ABOUT THEM. Sparkling has provided me with a unique way to give hope to those who are stressed and struggling. With your clear intention, sparkling can calm anxiety and worries. Your light-filled communication is a gift, supporting the threads of coherence and wholeness. Sparkling generates your energetic gifts with your loving compassion. According to Barbara De Angelis: "Love and kindness are never wasted. They always make a difference. They bless the one who receives them, and they bless you, the giver." Let me count the ways when I have applied sparkling. I have uplifted sad moods and spirits, given energetic support to wilting plants, blessed and protected my family and friends with light, upgraded impaired immune systems to meet health challenges, lowered the fear response, reinforced good habits and life changes, renewed self-love, boosted individual abundance, cleared chaotic energies and improved environmental conditions. It feels empowering to do something to help someone else. Sparkle when words are inadequate.

KEEP A SPARKLING JOURNAL. Record when you have sparkled someone, what your intentions were, how it felt, how it was received, and any highlights of sparkling moments throughout your day. I put my journal by my bed and write down my creative ideas to apply when I get the chance. I write down any synchronicities that have occurred or write about when I have felt the presence of other divine light helpers who are combining their light with mine. I note the accumulative effects of sparkling someone of something repeatedly over time.

INCORPORATE SPARKLING AS A SPIRITUAL APPROACH FOR MINDFULNESS. Through daily sparkling, my observation skills have gradually become more fine-tuned, because I am looking keenly at everything in the present moment. It's fun to discover little surprises as you notice that a flower displays a certain coloration, or an animal shows unique markings that brings unexpected delight and pleasure. Your increased awareness of the indescribable beauty that surrounds you brings great happiness, along with new insights, which elevate your frequency. Gratitude and awareness are the keys to your self-transformation. Find something beautiful and appreciate it.

PAY ATTENTION WHEN ENERGY APPEARS TO BE LOWERED. My senses now are keenly aware when things look dull and lifeless. Become attuned to notice if a person or plant has good life force or not and you can assist. Your sparkling engagement helps to replenish diminished energies and lighten up circumstances. As you go through each day, many things that can drain energies and lower your vibration, such as having an argument with a family member, or getting blocked in traffic, hearing bad news, getting sick, being a caregiver, dealing with drastic weather changes and being exposed to dense energies in a big store. Realize that life's challenges can deplete your energies more acutely in a modern world. Self-sparkling is a must!

DISCOVER CONTINUING REVELATIONS AS YOU APPLY THE ART OF SPARKLING. I have continued sparkling, even through times when it didn't seem to be working. I sparkle something or someone every day because I know how much it helps. My observation is that you generally see improvements over time. Do not be driven by results; be patient. My quest to sparkle better has opened me to realize and embody my divinity. I have both experienced and discovered unrealized realms of light that are available to each of us as we explore our inner capacities.

REMEMBER WHO YOU ARE. We are multidimensional energetic beings of light in physical bodies with quantum abilities. Keep this perspective in mind. Sparkling is an expressive art form that involves holding and increasing light in your body and biofields. This energetic acceleration expands your functioning and skillsets so that you can consciously enhance the beauty and health of life. You connect on body, mind, and spirit levels, leading you into spiritual growth. To my delight, this creative process has kept me evolving and changing in so many areas of my life. Over a decade of my sparkling journey, my entire being has expanded. I have felt the effects of exposure to greater thresholds of light that carry uplifting intelligence, which provide meaningful insights, with different levels of engagement.

EVOLVE YOUR LIGHT MASTERY! Your flowing sparkle power is your greatest asset for everything that you want to accomplish. It enables you to express your passion to serve life and progressively refines your skills with its creative and applied use. You will become illuminated as you sparkle life in a spirit of service. You enter a natural bliss state at a higher octave. Your own unique light can lovingly merge with other sources of light from other people and/or from higher dimensions to co-create collective momentum to uplift all life.

ACKNOWLEDGE THAT LIGHT IS THE MEDIUM FOR YOUR ARTISTIC PROCESS. As an artist, you sparkle with light as an energetic weaver, painter or dancer. You are the marvelous maestro who conducts light orchestras of higher energies that add the music of the spheres to create a sparkling harmonic creation. This mastery is not unlike the arts of baking bread, playing the piano, and arranging flowers, which were my grandmother's chosen virtuoso skills. The difference is that you sparkle energetically, without having your hands directly touch an object or person.

UNDERSTAND THAT EVERYTHING IS ENERGY. The science of sparkling is based on the new physics that allows you to understand why you are creating benefits. As Bruce H. Lipton states in *Biology of Belief*, "Atoms are made of invisible energy, not tangible matter!" We know that the energetic frequencies of light are always available. Cultivate your sparkling essence to increase your own frequencies and those of all living things. Choose to intentionally access the powerful waves of love and light that dwell within each of our hearts and within every cell. Others will be affected as we also share inter-connected heart intelligence. We carry divine inner technologies within us. We were created with these powerful resources as treasures to personally and collectively thrive and to help restore life.

You do not need spend a penny to do this. Your transmission of light is all you need. The art of sparkling is great news for the future of mankind.

> *"Intention appears to be something akin to tuning forks, causing the tuning forks of other things in the universe to resonate to the same frequency."*
>
> — Lynne McTaggart

Your Turn to Sparkle

"The artist does not bring the Divine on to the earth by letting it flow into the world. He raises the world into the Sphere of the Divine."

— Rudolf Steiner

I call on you to explore sparkling. Join with me and others to sparkle life to enhance the lives of others by showering them with scintillating, splendid light. *Learn this inspiring skill that increases your impact on those you love.* Now it's your turn to take the first step and decide who, what, and when to sparkle. Your intuition and imagination are your greatest resources.

This book has introduced you to a new quantum approach that allows you to move energies to raise the frequency of yourself, others and all living things. You have learned how to sparkle, using it as both an energetic tool and as a loving spiritual practice. Sparkling can be an everyday simple activity used and practiced with reverence for life. See for yourself the differences that you can make in the lives of others.

The sacred act of sparkling is a superpower that shines your divine spark like a beacon to share all the good in life. This skill has the potential to transform the seemingly impossible into the commonplace. Sparkling shifts consciousness to awaken the brilliant diamond sparkles of your bare-naked radiance, as love and light radiate from your pores and hands. Summon your whole being to energetically align with the highest expression of dazzling light available to you in each moment.

My own story reveals how I continuously received inspirational knowledge from brilliant teachers who shared their wisdom, and then created a new tool and spiritual practice that fully expressed the knowledge received. The funny part is that this ability was inside me all along, in an abiding way, waiting to be discovered, to teach others to shine even more brightly. Liberate your brilliance that dwells with you to shine like the most radiant diamonds. Sparkling connected me to my higher Divine purpose and can do the same for you perhaps.

As I gradually became a master of sparkling, I deepened my connection to my inner light that is infinite, existing everywhere. Applying this light reverently is a blessing that seems to improve everything. *Know that quantum potentials of light are available.* Use your hands and loving heart, aligned with your intuition to create positive change. I have developed distinct sensitivities to the energies around me, and can feel, touch and celebrate the distinct vibrations that exist at differing frequencies and bandwidths of Light. You can optimize your interconnection to other expansive fields of Light that can assist your offering of services. I grew in the knowing that there are vast networks of light beings who are guides, masters and angels. They serve as resources for your sparkling when you contact them or call on them for assistance.

I want to share some visualizations that may assist you on your sparkling journey. Let your imagination encourage you as you develop crystal clear images of yourself as a light-filled vessel. Your creativity is also encouraged, and you begin to think out of the box and discover new applications. I have found that using guided imagery helps raise your personal vibration. You glow after doing them and get more inspired to use your sparkling skills. Here are some ideas:

CALL ON THE LIGHT TO:

Brighten your presence with inspiring thoughts.

Bring the golden rays of the sun into your crown chakra. Direct this penetrating bright light through your entire body from head to toe for an energetic boost. Imagine a double helix that carries sunlight down through your entire body and sends starlight right back up.

Send swirling light around your body to create full body protection.

Receive a sparkling golden orb or shining disco ball filled with brilliant light that envelops your entire body. Allow it to fill you up with replenishing energies! Feel yourself energetically recreated and strengthened in your muscles, nerves, tissues, cells and organs.

Wake up to glorious morning light that sets a very positive tone for your day.

Breathe in the Purest Light to:

Receive enlivening energies.

Clear your entire being. Then exhale and release everything that does not belong.

Open and expand the light in your chakras. Allow them to shine brightly into a greater spinal column light that encompasses your whole body and energetic fields into One Unified Field of Light.

Shine like the sun as you expand into a huge ball of golden light.

Experience a perfect and complete metamorphosis that fully transforms you into a source of sparkling Light.

IMAGINE:

Wearing a magical, golden sparkling cloak that automatically clears your energies. It surrounds you with pure light that renews and amplifies happiness, security and abundance.

Standing under a shower that drenches you in the perfect color/frequencies that you need in the moment, leaving all your systems purified and rejuvenated.

Shining like a Christmas tree with hundreds of sparkling lights on every bough.

Surrounding yourself with nurturing circles of your families of Light in the Heavens, who may be religious figures, Divine Feminine Goddesses of Light, Angels, Star Beings, or loved ones who have passed on. They send you unconditional love and sparkle you with the purest Love and Light.

Glowing as a pillar of Golden White Light that extends to the Heavens and surrounds your body and biofields.

Traveling and living in a new world with sparkling air, shimmering atmospheres, and landscapes, with light-filled structures, populated with animals and people of all ages radiating health and happiness.

I hope these visualizations are helpful as you become a more sparkling version of yourself—head to toe. As you picture your glowing presence, you can be inspired to practice sending light transmissions out into the world to spread the word about sparkling. Combine the art of visualization; sparkling helps your beautiful light shine the brightest.

BECOME A LIGHT BEARER FOR HUMANITY!

Focus on this ideal. See yourself holding an illuminated torch. Your dedication strengthens your intent to use your inherent light abilities for the health and transformation of our planet. Light the path for others to create true magic and miracles to transform our world. With teamwork, we can use our quantum capabilities to set in motion the awakening of many souls to their innate light-filled, energetic abilities, beyond technology.

The light is needed now more than ever in a troubled world. The time is now to become a trailblazer for new beginnings to catalyze positive change. Let's envision thousands of us sparkling as a collective for the evolution of our planet, toward greater light.

As Mahatma Gandhi encouraged, "You must be the change that you wish to see in the world." How Divine to see a gathering of human sparklers bringing forth a resonant collective field by the anchoring and expressing of light and love. We can become human fireflies in sync, sparkling our world in all seasons. As free-spirited sparklers focused on light activities, we can build up the energetic intensity to "light up a city." Try sparkling to help make this dream become a shining bright reality.

> *"Even this late it happens:*
> *the coming of love, the coming of light.*
> *you wake and the candles are lit as if by themselves,*
> *stars gather, dreams pour into your pillows,*
> *sending up warm bouquets of air.*
> *Even this late the bones of the body shine*
> *and tomorrow's dust flares into breath."*
>
> — Mark Strand, *The Coming of Light*

Sparkling blessings

To Susanna Bensinger, my lifetime supporter, you who gave me my roots to magnify my star power.

To my beloved children, Brittain and Betsy, and to all my grandchildren, you light up my life every day! Sparkling and loving you all forever!

To my devoted husband, Eric, who is my writing companion, you are my sunshine and my first sparkle!

To my great teachers, you carried the torch of wisdom to allow me to teach my truth.

To Marcia Meier, my editor, publisher and friend, you gracefully helped me finish this book.

ABOUT THE AUTHOR

Becky Brittain, Ph.D., R-DMT, is a passionate sparkler of life. She is a clinically trained psychotherapist, life coach, registered dance-movement therapist, and energy transmitter.

Becky has a doctorate in prenatal and perinatal psychology from the Santa Barbara Graduate Institute, a master's degree in dance therapy from UCLA, and a bachelor's degree from Mount Holyoke College. For twenty-nine years, she was an adjunct lecturer in somatic psychology at Washington University in St. Louis.

She lives in Carpinteria, California.

Visit her at danceinlight.com

CPSIA information can be obtained
at www.ICGtesting.com
Printed in the USA
LVHW04203829082O
664253LV00006B/572